1

This book belongs to:

_____

Gemini Daily Horoscope 2023

Gemini Daily Horoscope 2023

Gemini

2023

JANUARY

M	T	W	T	F	S	S
						1
2	3	4	5	6	7	8
9	10	11	12	13	14	15
16	17	18	19	20	21	22
23	24	25	26	27	28	29
30	31					

FEBRUARY

M	T	W	T	F	S	S
		1	2	3	4	5
6	7	8	9	10	11	12
13	14	15	16	17	18	19
20	21	22	23	24	25	26
27	28					

MARCH

M	T	W	T	F	S	S
		1	2	3	4	5
6	7	8	9	10	11	12
13	14	15	16	17	18	19
20	21	22	23	24	25	26
27	28	29	30	31		

APRIL

M	T	W	T	F	S	S
					1	2
3	4	5	6	7	8	9
10	11	12	13	14	15	16
17	18	19	20	21	22	23
24	25	26	27	28	29	30

MAY

M	T	W	T	F	S	S
1	2	3	4	5	6	7
8	9	10	11	12	13	14
15	16	17	18	19	20	21
22	23	24	25	26	27	28
29	30	31				

JUNE

M	T	W	T	F	S	S
			1	2	3	4
5	6	7	8	9	10	11
12	13	14	15	16	17	18
19	20	21	22	23	24	25
26	27	28	29	30		

JULY

M	T	W	T	F	S	S
					1	2
3	4	5	6	7	8	9
10	11	12	13	14	15	16
17	18	19	20	21	22	23
24	25	26	27	28	29	30
31						

AUGUST

M	T	W	T	F	S	S
	1	2	3	4	5	6
7	8	9	10	11	12	13
14	15	16	17	18	19	20
21	22	23	24	25	26	27
28	29	30	31			

SEPTEMBER

M	T	W	T	F	S	S
				1	2	3
4	5	6	7	8	9	10
11	12	13	14	15	16	17
18	19	20	21	22	23	24
25	26	27	28	29	30	

OCTOBER

M	T	W	T	F	S	S
						1
2	3	4	5	6	7	8
9	10	11	12	13	14	15
16	17	18	19	20	21	22
23	24	25	26	27	28	29
30	31					

NOVEMBER

M	T	W	T	F	S	S
		1	2	3	4	5
6	7	8	9	10	11	12
13	14	15	16	17	18	19
20	21	22	23	24	25	26
27	28	29	30			

DECEMBER

M	T	W	T	F	S	S
				1	2	3
4	5	6	7	8	9	10
11	12	13	14	15	16	17
18	19	20	21	22	23	24
25	26	27	28	29	30	31

2023 AT A GLANCE

Eclipses

Hybrid Solar – April 20th

Penumbral Lunar – May 5th

Annular Solar – October 14th

Partial Lunar -October 28th

Equinoxes and Solstices

Spring - March 20th 21:25

Summer - June 21st 14:52

Fall – September 23rd 06:50

Winter – December 22nd 03:28

Mercury Retrogrades

December 29th, 2022 Capricorn - January 18th Capricorn

April 21st Taurus – May 15th Taurus

August 23rd Virgo – September 15th Virgo

December 13th Capricorn - January 2nd, 2024 Sagittarius

2023 FULL MOONS

Wolf Moon: January 6th, 23:09

Snow Moon: February 5th, 18:30

Worm Moon March 7th, 12:40

Pink Moon: April 6th, 4:37

Flower Moon: May 5th, 17:34

Strawberry Moon: June 4th, 3:42

Buck Moon: July 3rd, 11:40

Sturgeon Moon: August 1st, 18:32

Blue Moon: August 31st, 1:36

Corn, Harvest Moon: September 29th, 9:58

Hunters Moon: October 28th, 20:23

Beaver Moon: November 27th, 9:16

Cold Moon: December 27th, 0:34

2023 INGRESSES

Mars Ingresses

Mar 25, 2023, 11:36	Mars enters Cancer
May 20, 2023, 15:24	Mars enters Leo
Jul 10, 2023, 11:34	Mars enters Virgo
Aug 27, 2023, 13:15	Mars enters Libra
Oct 12, 2023, 3:39	Mars enters Scorpio
Nov 24, 2023, 10:10	Mars enters Sagittarius

Venus Ingresses

Jan 3, 2023, 2:06	Venus enters Aquarius
Jan 27, 2023, 2:29	Venus enters Pisces
Feb 20, 2023, 7:52	Venus enters Aries
Mar 16, 2023, 22:31	Venus enters Taurus
Apr 11, 2023, 4:43	Venus enters Gemini
May 7, 2023, 14:20	Venus enters Cancer
Jun 5, 2023, 13:42	Venus enters Leo
Oct 9, 2023, 1:06	Venus enters Virgo
Nov 8, 2023, 9:27	Venus enters Libra
Dec 4, 2023, 18:48	Venus enters Scorpio
Dec 29, 2023, 20:21	Venus enters Sagittarius

Mercury Ingresses

Feb 11, 2023, 11:22	Mercury enters Aquarius
Mar 2, 2023, 22:49	Mercury enters Pisces
Mar 19, 2023, 04:22	Mercury enters Aries
Apr 3, 2023, 16:20	Mercury enters Taurus
Jun 11, 2023, 10:24	Mercury enters Gemini
Jun 27, 2023, 0:22	Mercury enters Cancer
Jul 11, 2023, 4:09	Mercury enters Leo
Jul 28, 2023, 21:29	Mercury enters Virgo
Oct 5, 2023, 0:06	Mercury enters Libra
Oct 22, 2023, 6:46	Mercury enters Scorpio
Nov 10, 2023, 6:22	Mercury enters Sagittarius
Dec 1, 2023, 14:29	Mercury enters Capricorn

Slower Moving Ingresses

Mar 7, 2023, 13:03	Saturn enters Pisces
Mar 23, 2023, 8:42	Pluto enters Aquarius
May 16, 2023, 17:01	Jupiter enters Taurus

The Moon Phases

- New Moon (Dark Moon)
- Waxing Crescent Moon
- First Quarter Moon
- Waxing Gibbous Moon
- Full Moon
- Waning Gibbous (Disseminating) Moon
- Third (Last/Reconciling) Quarter Moon
- Waning Crescent (Balsamic) Moon

● New Moon (Dark Moon)

The New Moon reveals what hides beyond the realm of everyday circumstances. It creates space to focus on contemplation and the gathering of wisdom. It is the beginning of the moon cycles. It is a time for plotting your course and planning for the future. It does let you unearth new possibilities when you tap into the wisdom of what is flying under the radar. You can embrace positivity, change, and adaptability. Harness the New Moon's power to set the stage for developing your trailblazing ideas. It is a Moon phase for hatching plans for nurturing ideas. Creativity is quickening; thoughts are flexible and innovative. Epiphanies are prevalent during this time.

● Waxing Crescent Moon

It is the Moon's first step forward on her journey towards fullness. Change is in the air, it can feel challenging to see the path ahead, yet something is tempting you forward. Excitement and inspiration are in the air. It epitomizes a willingness to be open to change and grow your world. This Moon often brings surprises, good news, seed money, and secret information. This Moon brings opportunities that are a catalyst for change. It tempts the debut of wild ideas and goals. It catapults you towards growth and often brings a breakthrough that sweeps in and demands your attention. Changes in the air inspiration weave the threads of manifestation around your awareness.

First Quarter Moon

The First Quarter Moon is when exactly half of the Moon is shining. It signifies that action is ready to be taken. You face a crossroads; decisive action clears the path. You cut through indecisiveness and make your way forward. There is a sense of something growing during this phase. Your creativity nourishes the seeds you planted. As you reflect on this journey, you draw equilibrium and balance the First Quarter Moon's energy before tipping the scales in your favor. You feel a sense of accomplishment of having made progress on your journey, yet, there is still a long way to go. Pause, take time to contemplate the path ahead and begin to nurture your sense of perseverance and grit as things have a ways to go.

Waxing Gibbous Moon

Your plans are growing; the devil is in the detail; a meticulous approach lets you achieve the highest result. You may find a boost arrives and gives a shot of can-do energy. It connects you with new information about the path ahead. The Moon is growing, as is your creativity, inspiration, and focus. It is also a time of essential adjustments, streamlining, evaluating goals, and plotting your course towards the final destination. Success is within reach; a final push will get you through. The wind is beneath your wings, a conclusion within reach, and you have the tools at your disposal to achieve your vision.

Full Moon

The Full Moon is when you often reach a successful conclusion. It does bring a bounty that adds to your harvest. Something unexpected often unfolds that transforms your experience. It catches you by surprise, a breath of fresh air; it is a magical time that lets you appreciate what your work has achieved. It is time for communication and sharing thoughts and ideas. It often brings a revelation eliminating new information. The path clears, and you release doubt, anxiety, and tension. It is a therapeutic and healing time that lets you release old energy positively and supportively.

Waning Gibbous (Disseminating) Moon

The Waning gibbous Moon is perfect for release; it allows you to cut away from areas that hold back true potential. You may feel drained as you have worked hard, journeyed long, and are now creating space to return and complete the cycle. It does see tools arrive to support and nourish your spirit. Creating space to channel your energy effectively and cutting away outworn regions creates an environment that lets your ideas and efforts bloom. It is a healing time, a time of acceptance that things move forward towards completing a cycle. This the casting off the outworn, the debris that accumulates over the lunar month is a vital cleansing that clears space and resolves complex emotions that may cling to your energy if not addressed.

Third (Last/Reconciling) Quarter Moon

This Moon is about stabilizing your foundations. There is uncertainty shifting sands; as change surrounds your life, take time to be mindful of drawing balance into your world. It is the perfect time to reconnect with simple past times and hobbies. Securing and tethering your energy does build a stable foundation from which to grow your world. It is time to take stock and balance areas of your life. Consolidating your power by nurturing your inner child lets you embrace a chapter to focus on the areas that bring you joy. It is not time to advance or acquire new goals. It's a restful phase that speaks of simple pastimes that nurture your spirit.

Waning Crescent (Balsamic) Moon

The Waning Crescent Moon completes the cycle; this Moon finishes the set. It lets you tie up loose ends, finish the finer details, and essentially creates space for new inspiration to flow into your world once the cycle begins again. The word balsamic speaks of healing and attending to areas that feel raw or sensitive. It is a mystical phase that reconnects you to the cycle of life. As the Moon dies away, you can move away from areas that feel best left behind. Focusing on healing, meditation, self-care, and nurturing one's spirit is essential during this Moon phase.

The Full Moon: How it can affect your star sign

The Full Moon shines a light on areas that seek adjustment or healing in your life.

The Full Moon is a time to bring awareness into your spirit of the areas that seek resolution or adjustment. Over time, the past can create emotional blockages in your life. The Full Moon forms a sacred space to process sensitive emotions and release the past's hold on your spirit.

This lunar vibration brings awareness to your spirit of how your emotions affect your daily life. When the Moon is complete, your emotional awareness magnifies, and you feel things more intensely in your everyday life.

The Full Moon brings a chance to go over inner terrain and connect with your intuition. She shines a light on areas that hold the most significant meaning in your life. This effect has a powerful impact on creativity, planning, and future life direction. Tuning in and listening to your gut instincts helps you strip away from areas that only cloud judgment and muddy your awareness.

Gemini: Expect a turning point or epiphany to improve interpersonal relationships. The Full Moon energizes communication and improves bonds in your life. Pay close attention to what services under the Full Moon. Expect sharp insights and hidden information to surface. Resolving sensitive emotions promotes stability that gets you back on track after your Full Moon healing finishes.

I use the 24-hour clock/military time.
Time set to Coordinated Universal Time Zone (UT±0)

I've noted Meteor Showers on the date they peak.

JANUARY

Sun	Mon	Tue	Wed	Thu	Fri	Sat
1	2	3	4	5	6	7
8	9	10	11	12	13	14
15	16	17	18	19	20	21
22	23	24	25	26	27	28
29	30	31				

NEW MOON

WOLF MOON

30 Friday

An outstanding opportunity arrives, bringing a direction that aligns with your future vision. It lets you carve out quality time to spend developing a passion project. It brings a new enterprise that offers a creative aspect. It draws beneficial foundations that are grounded and happy. Life becomes sweeter, and this restores balance. It brings an opportunity to collaborate with an artistic character.

31 Saturday

Today speaks of an extended time that brings celebration and joy flowing into your world. It gets a chance to catch up with your broader social clan. Reconnecting with your tribe draws light and vibrancy into your social life. You soon enter a happy phase of nurturing interpersonal bonds. New possibilities capture the essence of inspiration, and this has you exploring an endeavor that offers a collaborative approach.

1 Sunday ~ New Year's Day, Venus conjunct Pluto 5:24

Venus, the ruler of love, offers an abundant landscape when conjunct with Pluto. The energy of transformation surrounds your life, enabling you to advance your romantic life. Manifesting your happiness is on the agenda as you deepen romance and grow the potential possible in your love life. You begin to see what is possible when you expand the borders of your life.

2 Monday ~ Mercury sextile Neptune 6:53

This sextile attracts free-flowing and creative ideas that help you place the cherry on top of this year's plans and aspirations. You make a beeline for developing goals and getting involved with your broader community. It has you feeling optimistic about the prospects ahead. As you direct your energy towards expanding your life, you discover opportunities that help you prosper.

3 Tuesday ~ Venus ingress Aquarius 2:06, Quadrantids Meteors runs Jan 1st – 5th

New possibilities ahead bring news that lifts the barriers. It opens your life to a social aspect that draws harmony and joy. It lets you resolve outworn energy as you head towards a turning point that offers rising prospects. It brings a lighter, happier phase of focusing on an area that holds meaning. Positive influences surge your social life and get a heightened sense of security that nurtures well-being and stability.

4 Wednesday ~ Venus sextile Jupiter 9:07

This sextile attracts warm and abundant energy into your social life. A dash of luck and good fortune combined with enriching conversations improve social bonds in your life. An opportunity ahead helps you redesign your life from the ground up. It connects you with kindred spirits who support growth. It offers a splash of color and a dynamic vibe that opens the gate towards growth and change. It brings a passage forward that marks the beginning of a new journey.

5 Thursday ~ Sun trine Uranus 16:43

This Sun trine Uranus transit brings positive change and excitement flowing into your world. An experimental flavor draws a new influence into your life. Reshuffling the decks of potential opens a curious path forward. It brings an emphasis on growing unique dreams and goals that offer expansion. Developments ahead let the puzzle pieces fall into place, creating a beautiful picture of what is possible when you believe in yourself.

6 Friday ~ Wolf Full Moon in Cancer 23:09

A time of self-discovery ahead helps you gain insights into areas best released. It also allows you to discover pathways that offer a ray of sunshine. Intuitive choices bring new possibilities into your life. It provides an essential phase of expansion, growth, and opportunity. Getting involved in creating a life of your making helps smooth over the rough edges and lets you set sail towards smoother sailing.

7 Saturday ~ Sun Conjunct Mercury 12:56

This conjunct bodes well for communication. Rising prospects draw insightful conversations that stimulate creativity and problem-solving mental energy. It has you spending time with friends and collaborating on developing goals and ideas. It brings a fruitful time that sees your social life shining brightly. Connecting with your circle of friends lays the groundwork for a joyful time that burns away sadness and ignites the fires of inspiration.

8 Sunday ~ Mercury trine Uranus 23:22

Mercury forming a trine with Uranus brings flashes of insight; expect an epiphany as brilliance surrounds your thought processes today. Your efforts to improve your circumstances bear fruit and offer a lush garden of opportunity. Discussions ahead bring a thoughtful vibe into your life. It releases stress and lets you flick anxiety to the curb. It enables you to get involved with an area that offers room to grow.

9 Monday ~ Venus trine Mars 15:21

This week, Venus trine Mars raises your energy and brings a vibrant passion for life. Opening your life to new possibilities brings an active environment ahead. Expanding the borders of your world brings a pleasing result that nurtures a more creative and expressive tone. Working with your talents and leaning into your strengths helps shape your goals and create the right environment from which to blossom.

10 Tuesday

Vast potential surrounds the periphery of your life. Exploring new options lets you create forward momentum that helps you develop goals. It brings change and progression, letting you build your world in an efficient and rewarding fashion. Riding a wave of promising energy opens the floodgates to rising potential in your life. You explore developing pursuits that offer excellence.

11 Wednesday

The more you work with your talents, the more you advance your gifts to the next level. Creating a daily practice for studying, researching, and developing your abilities gives you the best bet to achieve a winning trajectory. Your efforts to improve your skills bear fruit. Being open to unique pathways grows your life in an eclectic direction. As you paint the backdrop of your vision for future growth, you discover it offers room to extend your abilities.

12 Thursday ~ Mars turns direct 20:54

With the planet Mars moving forward, your energy, passion, and drive return full force. An influx of news opens a fresh chapter that brings a chance to rejuvenate and reboot your abilities in an enterprising area. Making your life a priority hits a sweet tune for your life. Listening to the music within your soul attracts an expressive and inspiring journey that aligns with destiny.

13 Friday ~ Sun sextile Neptune 14:11

The Sun brings light to your dreams. This energetic aspect offers a path that glitters with possibilities. Some positive news is looming overhead. A new approach takes prominence and brings a time of expanding your life outwardly. It brings people into your circle who provide insight, advice, and ideas. Blending the energies with friends brings a new possibility to light. It marks a time of exploring options and getting involved with a group project.

14 Saturday

News ahead helps you settle into a grounded groove that offers a new approach to life. It brings a focus on rising well-being and happiness as you direct your attention towards areas that hold the most significant meaning in your life. It brings social opportunities that add richness and warmth to your world. A time of lively discussions brings a vibrant flavor into your life as the path ahead clears and you get busy with a time of expansion.

15 Sunday ~ Venus square Uranus 1:21, Last Quarter Moon in Libra 2:12

A Venus Uranus square creates a need to balance and harmonize interpersonal bonds while honoring your need for freedom and expression. Significant changes ahead see life brimming with new energy. It offers a lighter chapter that nurtures more abundance and happiness in your world. Improvements are incoming for your social life. It brings a bright and beautiful time that lights up a sunny destination in your world.

16 Monday ~ Martin Luther King Day

Today brings fun, happiness, and joy into your surroundings. It lets you embrace the finer aspects of life. It brings a pleasing result that sees life improve in social connection matters. It brings an enviable element that lights up new potential. Kicking away the cobwebs, you embark on an adventurous time of flying high with kindred spirits. It sets a positive trend that leaves you feeling rejuvenated and refreshed.

17 Tuesday

A unique path calls your name, and expanding horizons brings a new approach that draws pleasing outcomes. You blend innovative thinking with refreshing ideas, and this sparks a winning combination that offers rising prospects. You see promising signs that you head towards growing your life outwardly. It brings a time bursting at the seams with new options.

18 Wednesday ~ Mercury turns direct 13:12

Mercury is the messenger planet of communication, collaboration, and creative expression. Life becomes more manageable and flows more easily during Mercury's direct phase. It helps you enter a prosperous cycle of expanding your circle of friends. It brings a highly expressive and connected time that nurtures well-being and harmony in your life. It opens the door to communicating with others.

19 Thursday

You are on track to reveal improvement, bringing grounded energy that helps smooth out the bumps. You reach a turning point and create space for releasing sensitive areas. News on the horizon encourages you to walk a path that aligns with your spirit. You discover a journey that is soul-affirming and rewarding. Exploring various avenues opens a way that brings a shift towards growth.

20 Friday ~ Sun ingress Aquarius 8:26

Creating space to nurture your life draws stability and balance into your world. It clears the deck to explore learning new areas and develop your abilities. It brings the chance to create an assignment that showcases your skills and gets your work to a broader audience. A spotlight on working with your creative abilities brings valuable rewards that sustain and nurture your spirit.

21 Saturday ~ New Moon in Aquarius 20:54

A busy time ahead focuses on building security. You reveal new options that expand horizons as you peel back the layers. It brings inspired possibilities that nurture small changes that add substantial benefits. Being proactive helps you develop a winning path towards a lively chapter of social engagement. Sharing with friends weaves golden threads of potential around your life. Lively discussions replenish emotional tanks and nurture well-being in your world.

22 Sunday ~ Venus conjunct Saturn 22:12, Uranus turns direct 23:23
Chinese New Year (Rabbit)

The Chinese New Year heralds good luck and fortune. Rabbits are a symbol of growth and fertility. Ideas planted in fertile terrain will get a chance to blossom and grow. You become more confident about chasing your vision and developing your goals. New leads offer a path that supports growth and advancement. You deepen the potential by being open to further possibilities.

23 Monday

Creating space to nurture your talents draws a positive shift forward. It brings a journey that marks a significant turning point in your life. It gives you insight into future possibilities. A richly creative process is at the crux of this path, and exploring the options lets you work with your abilities and refine your gifts. A unique landscape tempts you forward as new priorities soon take shape.

24 Tuesday

Working with creativity anchors you in a grounded environment that restores equilibrium. It opens the book on a unique chapter that lets you use your abilities to establish an enterprising journey forward. Abundance is a theme that resonates strongly around your surroundings as you explore pathways that offer rising prospects in your life. It brings an enriching time that provides a fresh start as you connect with a compelling journey.

25 Wednesday ~ Sun sextile Jupiter 1:30

In sextile with Jupiter, the Sun attracts a restless vibe that has you yearning to expand your life outwardly. Good fortune lights a shimmering path forward that has you eager to set out on a new journey. Beautiful changes arrive to tempt you out and about with others of a similar mindset. Life offers a refreshing social aspect that brings people into your world. Exploring new pathways brings joy.

26 Thursday

The more proficient you become at your job, the more your confidence rises. It has you feeling ready to seek new opportunities that offer expansion in your life. It brings pathways of growth that offer rising prospects. You undertake to develop your talents and expand your abilities. It brings a path that promotes your skills and extends your reach into a new area. A new role helps bring your gifts to a broader audience.

27 Friday ~ Venus ingress Pisces 2:29

You will soon tap into opportunities that help you share your talents with others. Being open to upgrading your life in this manner leaves you feeling energized and ready to tackle ambitious projects to advance life. You soon discover options that enable you to build impressive foundations that improve your bottom line. Being flexible and adaptable helps you pivot on a dime and set sail wherever the wind calls your name.

28 Saturday ~ First Quarter Moon in Taurus 15:19

You can expect extra opportunities to mingle. A social aspect brings a journey that advances life towards a wellspring of potential. It gets a lovely boost as you foster developing personal bonds that lead to companionship. It liberates your mood with a freedom-loving environment that captures the essence of adventure. Manifestation gently weaves magic through your life by restoring well-being and promoting harmony in your world.

29 Sunday

Turning your attention towards your social life draws a rewarding chapter of improving circumstances. It creates a bridge towards a lighter and more connected future. Lively discussions offer a productive journey that supports your world as it nurtures well-being. It gives you a solid base to grow your circle of friends. It connects you with companions who feed your inspiration with fresh ideas.

FEBRUARY

Sun	Mon	Tue	Wed	Thu	Fri	Sat
			1	2	3	4
5	6	7	8	9	10	11
12	13	14	15	16	17	18
19	20	21	22	23	24	25
26	27	28				

NEW MOON

SNOW MOON

30 Monday ~ Sun trine Mars 1:45, Mercury trine Uranus 2:17
Mercury at Greatest Eastern Elongation: 25.0°W

It is a productive time that opens the doors to new possibilities. It gives you a chance to work with your talents; it draws an expressive and favorable path that highlights movement around your career path. It draws an assignment that offers impressive results. Focusing on a project ripe for progression attracts new possibilities that glide your working life towards growth.

31 Tuesday

A busy time ahead lets you sort through options and choose an area of interest. Something is on offer soon, and it lands you in a different landscape. It brings an active phase of developing unique potential. Expansion shifts your focus forward, which helps you sidestep issues and leave them in the tailwind of your progress. The essence of wanderlust captures an exciting journey that offers room to grow your world.

1 Wednesday ~ Imbolc

You soon make good headway around developing your goals. It brings a lucky break that you have worked hard to accomplish. A door opens towards advancing your life into a prestigious new area. A focused effort to improve your circumstances draws dividends. It lets you navigate a complex strategy and come out on top. Developments ahead allow the pieces of your puzzle to fall into place, setting the stage to nurture your abilities.

2 Thursday~ Groundhog Day

An aspect ahead gives you opportunities to grow a fascinating path forward. It brings a grounded environment that helps you develop a promising area. It may have you rethinking long-term plans as a new trajectory calls your name. It takes you to a radiant time of nurturing your gifts of creativity and innovation. It brings magic and growth, which kickstarts a refreshing time of expanding your world as you pour your energy into a worthwhile area.

3 Friday

A sparkling time draws communication. It brings a creative aspect that kicks off a journey that motivates change. It adds to your sense of security and happiness as you build foundations that secure a path forward. Life hums along and brings news of a venture that leads to growth. It places a focus on building skills and working with your gifts. It brings the correct elements into your world that help you thrive.

4 Saturday ~ Sun square Uranus 2:50

This positive square offers rising creativity that cultivates a new approach. Indeed, new options light a fire in your belly. It sparks a journey that provides growth, excitement, and expansion. You are ready to nurture a new area, directing your energy towards your vision, lights a path worth exploring. Life heads to an upswing as a prosperous cycle emerges in the future looks rosy. Opportunity is looming, bringing new horizons into view.

5 Sunday ~ Venus square Mars 3:28, Snow Full Moon in Leo 18:30

This square can cause challenges as a difference of opinion fosters tension and conflict. Being flexible, understanding, and adaptive will help harmonize bonds and limit the disruption caused by Venus facing Mars at a harsh angle. Being willing to compromise will improve the foundations and limit the disruption in your life. It brings a time of letting go of areas that restrict progress.

6 Monday ~ Mercury sextile Neptune 18:27

Rational thinking and dreams align in this sextile. You see rising creativity and analytical thinking promoting epiphanies that count. This cosmic alignment helps your dreams become a reality as structured backing behind your vision offers tangible results. It clarifies the path ahead as options pop up to support developing goals. You turn the tides in your favor and draw unique possibilities into your life. It brings a dream of yours into focus.

7 Tuesday

Changes ahead bring a turning point that liberates stress and worry. It brings a prime time for developing career goals and heading towards growth and advancement. Creativity rises as you transition towards learning new areas. It brings a busy time that launches your talents and raises the potential around your life. It ushers in unique opportunities to develop an enterprising area. As you tip the scales in your favor, you soon discover room to progress goals.

8 Wednesday ~ Venus sextile Uranus 5:28

Spontaneity, fun, and fresh adventures rule your social life with this engaging sextile. It sets the trend to improve your social life as it gets a sunny aspect that puts the spotlight on interpersonal bonds. The tide turns in your favor, offering a fresh start that provides stability and harmony. It brings a lucky break that offers curious new dreams. Sharing with kindred spirits draws a replenishing vibe that restocks inspiration.

9 Thursday

You head to a time of growth that advances your talents into a new area. An impressive lead lands in your lap and gets the ball rolling on developing your skills. The more you work on improving the path ahead, the more fate comes to meet you with new opportunities and projects worth your time. A richly creative process is at the crux of this journey; exploring new pathways brings possibilities to contemplate. Working with your abilities improves life from the ground up.

10 Friday ~ Mercury conjunct Pluto 17:16

Today's conjunct between Mercury and Pluto offers intense curiosity to delve a little deeper into life's mysteries. Life provides pearls of wisdom that give you insight into a deeper reality. It provides access to more profound truths that creates space to nurture a spiritual path. It brings an enriching time immersing yourself in an area of interest. It underscores rising meaning in your life.

11 Saturday ~ Mercury ingress Aquarius 11:22

News arrives to tempt you forward. Life picks up speed and heads towards a dynamic and engaging time catching up with friends. Opportunities ahead bring happiness flowing into your life. You head to an extensive chapter that reinvents the potential in your life. It positions you correctly to grow your personal life and expand your world outwardly. It offers a dynamic landscape that nurtures a wellspring of potential.

12 Sunday

Taking a moment to reflect on the past helps process sensitive emotions that hold you back from achieving your highest yield. Releasing the baggage brings healing flowing into your world. It lets you set your future intentions and develop the path ahead in alignment with the person you are becoming. Channeling your energy into a journey that holds meaning offers an inspiring way forward.

13 Monday ~ Last Quarter Moon in Scorpio 16:01

You discover possibilities that promote growth and advancement. A curious option arrives and draws lighter energy. It offers a breakthrough that sees you focusing your efforts on a big-picture goal. Lifting the shutters on an enterprising time of discovery creates a wellspring of abundance as you open the path ahead towards growth. You discover a penchant for creative areas that deepen your knowledge and expand your skillset.

14 Tuesday ~ Valentine's Day

Your life enjoys an upward trend, and this brings a boost. You move in alignment with an abundant landscape, and this brings much-needed clarity into personal goals. Focusing on your social life opens a path that holds the key to future happiness. It gets a chance to deepen a bond that inspires harmony and romance. It offers a refreshing social aspect that hits a high note in your personal life.

15 Wednesday ~ Venus conjunct Neptune 12:25

Venus joins forces with Neptune, and your love life takes on a dreamy quality as you engage in fanciful thoughts and contemplation. The desire moves into the realm of unlimited imagination as you think about the future, intending to nurture romance in your life. It brings a happy and pleasure-driven chapter that promotes a loving bond. Rough edges that caused friction in your love life soon smooth out, bringing an abundant landscape.

16 Thursday ~ Saturn conjunct Sun 16:48

Saturn connects with the Sun to blaze a trail towards developing your goals. Getting serious about limiting distractions and cultivating discipline, concentration, and order will help you nail progress in your working life. Gaining traction on improving the security in your world will bring a valuable sense of achievement and accomplishment to your door.

17 Friday

You explore a path that heightens your abilities. It allows room to evolve into a new pathway of growth and learning. It brings a journey that is inspiring, trailblazing, and eclectic. Life gets a reboot, taking you towards a chapter of nurturing your talents. Being flexible opens the floodgates to grounding energy that restores balance. A goal comes to life that sparks a shift forward.

18 Saturday ~ Mercury sextile Jupiter 2:13, Sun ingress Pisces 22:30

The Mercury Jupiter aspect creates harmony between both planets. It sparks rising curiosity, questioning, and fresh ideas, focusing on self-development and growth. It helps you take a big step forward and embark on a journey that develops your vision. Signs and serendipity help guide the path along. It draws a generous and abundant chapter for your life.

19 Sunday ~ Venus sextile Pluto 17:04

Today's Venus and Pluto alignment offers depth and insight into your thought processes. It helps you dig a little deeper and discover what drives your passion. Thinking about the areas that hold the most significant meaning in your life can be helpful on many levels. It weeds out the areas that no longer are a good fit for your life by letting you see the most meaningful aspects of your world. Moving in alignment with the person you are becoming nurtures inspiration.

20 Monday ~ Presidents' Day. New Moon in Pisces 7:08, Venus ingress Aries 7:52

Life attracts a new array of possibilities. Friends seek you out; social engagement is on the rise. It brings an interest in new areas and offers pathways towards growth. It leads to a richly creative and expressive environment that draws a pleasing result. It sets up a stable foundation that helps progress your situation outwardly. It draws lengthy conversations that let you head towards a happy chapter.

21 Tuesday ~ Shrove Tuesday (Mardi Gras), Mercury square Uranus 22:22

Original thinking, creative brainstorming, and insightful epiphanies are the order of the day as Mercury squares off against Uranus today. Something new and inspiring flows into your life. Exciting news ahead brings a fresh opportunity to ponder. You enter a cycle of optimistic expression that sees things falling into place. It brings an original and lively adventure that puts the wind back in your sails.

22 Wednesday ~ Ash Wednesday, Lent Begins, Mercury trine Mars 20:14

A Mercury trine Mars aspect attracts a restless vibe. This cosmic alignment leaves you feeling spontaneous and ready for new adventures today. It links you to a path that brings gifts and luck. It captures the essence of wanderlust and offers an exciting journey forward. A creative aspect helps bring artistic expression out in the open. An expressive and trailblazing time following your heart begins a positive trend that expands your life.

23 Thursday

You are ready to improve your bottom line and soon set off on developing a lofty goal. Life picks up steam, and new possibilities offer dynamic potential that brings the room to grow your talents. A magic option lets you create space to nurture creativity by getting involved in a new area. It brings a foundation that offers a stable basis to journey towards growth. The right conditions expand options, and this hits a sweet note.

24 Friday

You soon gain insight into the path ahead. It brings an opportunity that lets you step into your power and achieve a magnificent result. It brings new options that keep life humming along sustainably and progressively. It sets the stage to develop a situation that inspires change. The borders of your life expand and give you an exciting glimpse of future possibilities.

25 Saturday

A creative journey beckons your heart. It lets you work with your talents and immerse yourself in a productive environment. It glides you towards a relaxing scene that nurtures well-being and favors expansion in your social life. It places you well to improve your circumstances when new information reaches you. It brings a forward-facing chapter to light that offers progression

26 Sunday

Changes coming up draw social engagement. It breaks old patterns and ways of thinking by connecting you with unique people and potential. It marks the beginning of an inspiring journey that offers new adventures with kindred spirits. It propels you toward an encouraging environment that provides room to grow your circle of friends. It brings lively discussions and sharing of ideas.

MARCH

Sun	Mon	Tue	Wed	Thu	Fri	Sat
			1	2	3	4
5	6	7	8	9	10	11
12	13	14	15	16	17	18
19	20	21	22	23	24	25
26	27	28	29	30	31	

NEW MOON

WORM MOON

27 Monday ~ First Quarter Moon in Gemini 8:06

Creativity is key to expanding horizons in your life. It is wise to invest in yourself and your abilities as you have a lot to contribute to a broader audience. Sharing your gifts opens a clear path that brings a fresh wave of potential into your life. It brings cohorts and kindred spirits who offer support and guidance. It draws innovative solutions that see you working with your creativity to advance life into new areas.

28 Tuesday

Doing research and exploring new pathways brings high-level options into your life. Opportunities ahead offer a newfound project that becomes a source of inspiration. It brings rising motivation that opens the way towards growth in your life. It ushers in an impressive social aspect that cultivates lively discussions, engagement, and sharing with insightful companions.

1 Wednesday

Staying flexible and adaptable helps you weather any storms and head towards advancement. Pushing back the barriers ultimately improves foundations. A transformational aspect highlights golden opportunities ahead. Staying open to new opportunities and connecting with people who feed and nourish your spirit draws a positive outcome.

2 Thursday ~ Venus conjunct Jupiter 17:35, Mercury conjunct Saturn 14:34, Mercury ingress Pisces 22:49

Today's Venus conjunct Jupiter aspect is a positive sign for your social life. Expect an upward trend as rising prospects draw communication and invitations to mingle. Friendships blossom and the sense of companionship and support are rewarding. It brings a time of heart-to-heart communication that offers room to grow your social life.

3 Friday

A social aspect ahead produces dramatic results for your life. It brings a sense of connection that sparkles brightly and has you feeling valued. It places you in the proper alignment to nurture interpersonal bonds. It brings renewal and rejuvenation as you embrace a chance to catch up with friends. It provides the appropriate arena to discuss ideas and future-facing topics with friends and colleagues.

4 Saturday

Being open to change marks a significant turning point that sees potential skyrocket in your life. It brings a bounty of new options to shift your focus forward. It offers a great harvest as it brings the cream to the top. It lights up pathways towards teamwork and technology. Expanding your reach through networking and mingling keeps you in touch with kindred spirits who offer cutting-edge ideas and insightful dialogues.

5 Sunday

You enter a new growth cycle where you can build stable foundations and head towards unique opportunities that call your name. Information arrives that cracks the code to the chapter ahead. Changes in the air align to help you transition forward. A slow but steady transformation improves the foundations of your world. As events unfold, you bring an enriching chapter to light that sees emotional well-being soaring.

6 Monday ~ Purim (Begins at sundown), Sun sextile Uranus 13:41

This sextile heightens creativity and self-expression. You discover a new approach that boosts productivity and offers efficiency in your daily life. Change and discovery add a spontaneous element today. Anything could crop up to provide you with newfound inspiration. You can make yourself a priority and tap into creative pathways that encourage growth and evolve your abilities. It opens a chapter of new beginnings that expand your life.

7 Tuesday ~ Worm Full Moon in Virgo 12:40 Purim (Ends at sunset), Saturn ingress Pisces 13:03

The planet Saturn moving into Pisces is a significant shift. This changing of the Saturnian guards highlights the need for spiritual healing. It emphasizes finding meaning in your daily life and growing a solid spiritual basis to help you ride out any turbulence in your life. The path ahead offers wisdom. It allows you to move away from a difficult chapter and build new foundation blocks.

8 Wednesday

An enterprising area offers exciting prospects that become part of a more extensive chapter of growth in your life. It leads to developing new interests and goals. Serendipity lights the way ahead, bringing an uptick of possibility. It smooths over the rough edges of your life and brings companionship. Life ahead lines up to support your efforts to improve circumstances.

9 Thursday

Good news flows into your life. It helps you lay the groundwork to improve the security in your world. Focusing on advancing your vision for future growth lets you make the essential changes that offer rising prospects in your working life. Your willingness to explore leads brings a positive result. It opens the gateway towards growth in your working life. You soon get busy developing skills and learning the path ahead.

10 Friday

A golden opportunity emerges and brings lightness flowing into your life. It removes roadblocks that hinder progress and provides you with an open path towards chasing dreams and engaging in a more social and abundant landscape. It draws an environment that is enriching and meaningful. New energy flows into your life and brings the sharing with friends in a relaxing and soothing atmosphere.

11 Saturday ~ Venus sextile Mars 15:04, Mercury sextile Uranus 21:04

Venus has your back today and draws social engagement into your life. It opens the floodgates to an enriching time that brings invitations to circulate with friends and kindred spirits. It offers a beautiful adventure that nurtures your social life and helps you move toward a destination that inspires your world. It draws a stable foundation and brings an active phase of lively conversations and opportunities to mingle.

12 Sunday

Keeping your energy open helps achieve growth in your life. Dissolving blocks creates space for new possibilities to flourish. News arrives that sparks a journey of growth, learning, and wisdom. It puts the shine on your abilities and brings an enriching chapter to light. It marks a time of shifting your energy forward as you feed the creativity within and heighten the potential possible in your world.

13 Monday

News arrives that brings a sudden change. There is an opportunity to grow, which brings a role that is a perfect fit for your life. It delivers a cycle that puts your vision in motion. It brings the correct potential, leading to a dynamic development phase. Sunny skies emerge; your focus is on achieving the highest result. Look for signs and messages; the good news is coming soon.

14 Tuesday

You discover an open road of exciting options that tempt you forward. It brings a burst of sunshine into your world. It offers new possibilities that help you power ahead using skills and abilities. Newfound motivation fuels inspiration and enables you to launch into a new chapter of significant gains for your life. It leads to a richly creative environment that sets up a stable foundation from which to grow your life outwardly.

15 Wednesday ~ Last Q Moon in Sagittarius 2:08, Sun conjunct Neptune 23:39

You may feel sensitivities rising today as the Sun links up with Neptune in the sign of Pisces today. Intuition is sparking, and you can trust your gut instincts to guide you correctly when you reveal curious information that triggers your emotions. You make a decision that opens a path worth developing. It plants the seeds that offer room to revolutionize your life from the ground up.

16 Thursday ~ Mercury conjunct Neptune 17:13, Sun square Mars 18:09, Venus square Pluto 19:58, Venus ingress Taurus 22:31

Today, you may feel chaotic and under pressure as a great deal of cosmic energy disrupts stability in your life. Expect intensity as the Sun square Mars alignment may leave you feeling tense and hot under the collar. Creative expression and taking time to make yourself a priority will be beneficial in releasing frustrations and any heavy energy clinging to your spirit.

17 Friday ~ St Patrick's Day. Mercury square Mars 4:48,
Sun conjunct Mercury 10:45, Venus sextile Saturn 20:25

Today, Venus sextile Saturn promotes cooperation and offers the chance to join a joint project. As you make notable tracks on improving your circumstances, you can appreciate how far you have traveled on this journey. Something on offer soon sparks your interest and opens the gate to a new chapter of potential. An insightful person shares advice, bringing collaboration into focus.

18 Saturday

A focus on interpersonal ties brings communication flowing into your social life. It offers fun and friendship ahead as an active and dynamic environment fuels your desire to bond with your broader social circle. Life brings an opportunity to embrace as you move forward and spend time enjoying companionship in a social setting. It draws a path that offers significant growth and expansion.

19 Sunday ~ Mercury ingress Aries 4:22

A social aspect expands your horizons. It brings a vital transition that nurtures companionship and attracts good things into your life. You deepen a friendship with the thoughtful person who offers insightful ideas. Immersing yourself in a social environment balances your foundations. Communication and activities nourish your soul and connect with your tribe. Life brims with new possibilities to improve your world. You strike gold by getting involved with your social life.

20 Monday ~ Sun sextile Pluto 20:12, Sun ingress Aries 21:20, Ostara/Spring Equinox 21:25

News arrives, which offers a fresh start in your life. It helps you discover several significant opportunities currently circulating in the background of your life. A side adventure comes calling and brings a unique trail that nurtures your abilities and refines your talents. It helps you keep creative fires burning as inspiration sweeps in to encourage expansion. It offers an outlet that promotes your skills.

21 Tuesday ~ New Moon in Pisces 17:22

Creating a plan and mapping out your vision for future growth will help connect you with a journey that offers a positive result for your career path. Extending your reach into a new area enables you to cut away from areas that failed to reach fruition. Change is ahead, pointing you towards a path learning the ropes of a new role. New ideas, curiosity, and thirst for knowledge will be on the rise as you open your life up to developing unique areas that spark your interest.

22 Wednesday ~ Ramadan Begins

Advancement is in the pipeline. You are setting your sights on achieving your vision which charts a course towards growing your career path. It does reveal pathways that deepen your knowledge and develop your talents. As you transition towards learning a new area, you refine your abilities and connect with a vibrant landscape that offers growth and rising prospects. It does position you to advance your working life to the next level.

23 Thursday ~ Pluto ingress Aquarius 8:42

Moving onwards brings a surge of optimism that lets luck flow into your life. It brings a creative time of immersing yourself in developing new journeys for your life. Releasing the shadows and healing the past gets an open road of potential. It marks a freedom-driven journey that opens the floodgates to growing your life in a unique direction. Acting on instincts reveals refreshing options worth your time.

24 Friday

A more stable landscape emerges soon. It does bring a welcome shift forward that increases the potential possible. Life expands at a comfortable pace as you draw profitable opportunities that focus on improving your circumstances. It does let you embrace life-affirming endeavors that stabilize and bring balance into your environment. Friends tempt you out into the broader community.

25 Saturday ~ Mars ingress Cancer 11:36

You reach a turning point that creates space for unique possibilities to blossom in your world. It brings grounded energy that balances foundations and smooths over sensitive areas. It reawakens you to a sense of adventure that liberates your spirit and ushers in a freedom-loving vibe. A sense of rejuvenation wipes the slate clean as you shake off those heavy vibrations and release stress. A chapter of exciting possibilities tempts you towards expansive horizons.

26 Sunday

Changing priorities bring a new life cycle to light. You set your sights on developing new areas, and this brings a sense of excitement as you expand the barriers and head towards growth. New information surfaces that get a turning point. It offers a supportive vibe that connects you with kindred spirits. Being open to changing things up initiates a progressive and happy journey. Being in sync with your vision for future growth draws a pleasing outcome.

27 Monday

Information will arrive; that is a game-changer. It unleashes new possibilities that head you towards a time of growth. It motivates you to push past limitations and head towards an exciting vista of new options. Being receptive to change rejuvenates and re-energizes your spirit. You discover a journey that promotes wellness and harmony. It offers a vibrant time to nurture the foundations and develop social bonds.

28 Tuesday ~ Mercury conjunct Jupiter 6:49

This astrological conjunct is perfect for brainstorming as ideas are big and expressive under this planetary influence. You benefit from a whirlwind of activity overhead that supports learning. A dream comes into focus; nurturing this vision becomes the focal point. It helps you find balance in an uncertain world by focusing on goodness and leaving the rest behind. Creating stepping stones towards new goals draws security and harmony into your surroundings.

29 Wednesday ~ First Quarter Moon in Cancer 2:32

You are currently undergoing a transition that releases the past and allows new opportunities to enter your life. Dabbling in your interests shines a light on growing a creative enterprise. Working with your talents draws a nurturing influence that releases outworn areas and builds stable foundations that rebalance and rejuvenate your life. It soon translates to a fresh start that offers rising prospects.

30 Thursday ~ Mars trine Saturn 19:03, Venus conjunct Uranus 22:25

Mars forms a trine with Saturn today to give your working life wings. Hard work, dedication, and perseverance improve the day-to-day foundations of your life. Venus teams up with Uranus to add a dash of spontaneity to your social/personal life. As you set out on a new adventure, staying true to yourself will keep you aligned with the person you are becoming. With the wind beneath your wings, you navigate with ease towards unique pathways.

APRIL

Sun	Mon	Tue	Wed	Thu	Fri	Sat
						1
2	3	4	5	6	7	8
9	10	11	12	13	14	15
16	17	18	19	20	21	22
23	24	25	26	27	28	29
30						

New Moon

Pink Moon

31 Friday

Life moves from strength to strength as you develop the path onward. News arrives that brings a bright flavor to your life. It flings open the door to a journey that grows your situation in a new direction. It draws a prosperous time to connect with your circle of friends. Circulating in your wider community triggers a cascade of options that let you move forward towards developing companionship in your life.

1 Saturday ~ All Fools/April Fool's Day

Laying the foundations for improvement holds the key to a new growth cycle. Expanding opportunities offer a trailblazing journey forward towards rising prospects. A positive trend sees life pick up steam as new options emerge in your life. It brings a valuable reward for growing your life outwardly. Amid a time of change, you discover a journey that captures the essence of luck.

2 Sunday ~ Palm Sunday.

Fortune favors expansion, and life progresses towards an enriching time of developing unique goals. Re-evaluating your life offers a new outlook that marks a turning point. You refuel energy tanks and head off towards setting new goals that inspire your mind. The more you push back the barriers, the easier it becomes to assert yourself and pursue your dreams. It cultivates new options that break up stagnant patterns as you develop your skills to the next level.

3 Monday ~ Mercury ingress Taurus 16:20

It's a great time to nurture your life and create new foundations that stoke the fires of your imagination. A firm decision ahead brings a journey that offers abundance. Life holds a refreshing change as it provides movement and discovery. It brings a time of reshaping goals as the pace picks up momentum and you head towards a busy chapter. Advancement is in the pipeline, a new initiative comes calling.

4 Tuesday

Changes ahead bring new options that offer growth and stability. It helps you gain traction on developing goals as you discover an opportunity previously hidden from sight. Getting involved in cultivating your talents and working with your abilities brings a happy time that offers grounded and secure foundations. It lets you widen and grow your skills as you extend your reach to a new area. It removes the heaviness and ushers in lighter and more vibrant energy.

5 Wednesday ~ Passover (begins at sunset), Mercury sextile Saturn 16:18

With Mercury in sextile with Saturn, communication skills are rising. Enhanced clarity and mental insight help you understand more significant concepts, thought processes, and ideas with ease today. This cosmic enhancement enables you to step beyond traditional learning and take your studies/working life to the next level. It helps you pole vault over the hump day. Confidence is on the rise, enabling you to upgrade your life and meet any demands on the to-do list.

6 Thursday ~ Lent Ends. Pink Full Moon in Libra 4:37

Creating space for inner reflection can help you connect with insight and information. Weeding out distractions nurturing some quiet time enables you to hear the wisdom within. Something tempting arrives soon to breathe fresh air into your surroundings. It offers a soothing element that balances frazzled nerves and harmonizes your spirit. It brings a joyous shift that helps you break free of limiting patterns and enjoy an open road ahead.

7 Friday ~ Good Friday, Venus sextile Neptune 17: 59

Today's planetary alignment offers a mindful, spiritual aspect that is in keeping with the spirit of Easter. Venus sends loving beams into your home and family life, harmonizing bonds and drawing the essence of rejuvenation and renewal. It does improve the sense of connection in your life as a time of thoughtful conversations that connect the dots in a supportive environment. Sharing ideas brings expansive energy that encourages you to continue to develop your life.

8 Saturday ~ Mercury sextile Mars 6:23

A sextile between Mercury and Mars sharpens cognitive abilities today. Mental clarity is on the rise, giving you valuable insight into the path ahead. Stepping back to re-evaluate progress is essential; it brings a new perspective that marks a turning point. It enables you to refuel and renew your energy. It is a time of reflection, revision, tweaking, and planning.

9 Sunday ~Easter Sunday

News arrives, which inspires growth. It connects with sharing thoughts and ideas with those who understand your thinking and value your contribution. Rising creativity creates a brew of potential that offers increasing options. It brings a social aspect that nurtures stable foundations. Opportunities to socialize with friends bring a happy chapter.

10 Monday

A new possibility springs to life and points the way forward. It quickens the pace as further information offers a clean slate of potential. It gives you a leg up to an environment that provides connection, communication, and support. Your willingness to improve your circumstances brings a prosperous time of sharing thoughtful conversations. A productive and active time creates grounded foundations that nurture growth in your life.

11 Tuesday ~ Venus ingress Gemini 4:43, Venus trine Pluto 10:14,
Sun Conjunct Jupiter 22:07, Mercury at Greatest Elong 19.5E

A crossroads ahead brings a transition in your life. It is beneficial to listen to your inner guidance system during this transformation. Your intuition helps reveal new possibilities that draw stability, harmonize foundations, and bring a firm basis from which to grow your life. It offers an empowering time of exploring new options that spark creativity and magic.

12 Wednesday

You can expect extra opportunities ahead that nurture a sense of self-expression. It brings a creative aspect that builds a path of increasing stability. It releases uncertainty and lets you immerse your energy in an area that captures the essence of manifestation. It brings fullness and fertility to your creativity, bringing new options to contemplate. It offers a peak season for innovation, growth, and good luck.

13 Thursday ~ Passover (ends at sunset), Last Quarter Moon in Capricorn 9:11

A change of direction brings more incredible blessings into your life. It triggers a positive change that takes your vision further. A pathway opens for your social life; this becomes a strong focus for you moving forward. Nurturing your life brings expansion into view. It offers a fruitful time to increase your circle of friends. As you create headway on developing your life, you connect with a happy time ahead.

14 Friday ~ Orthodox Good Friday, Venus square Saturn 16:38

A Venus square Saturn encourages taking personal inventory of meaningful areas in your life. Adjusting course as necessary will give private bonds the best chance of success. You are shining an intensive light on interpersonal situations in your social life. It helps you cut away from toxic influences that limit you from reaching your highest trajectory. Not everyone is deserving of your time and attention. Saturn will help you trim the deadwood holding you back.

15 Saturday

Life takes on a rosy glow as you move forward towards new possibilities. It is a pivotal time to create change and open a new life cycle. Fresh beginnings leave you feeling inspired. Expansion around your social life kicks off an engaging and happy time of cultivating friendships and nurturing companionship. It brings invitations to circulate with friends, which hits a sweet note in your life.

16 Sunday ~ Orthodox Easter

Life settles into a more enriching phase that rewards you with growth. It refuels your emotional tanks and draws support as you deepen the potential possible in your life. Heightened security attracts grounded foundations that strengthen your life. You appreciate having abundant opportunities to explore development. The rollercoaster smooths out over time, drawing a positive outcome for your life.

17 Monday

Good news ahead lights the way forward for your working life. You lift the lid on an enterprising chapter that opens the gate to a big step up, and developing this area is worth your time. Rising prospects on the job front get good results your way. You begin building stable foundations that draw security and nurture a happy working environment. It gives you a leg up on a journey that offers advancement.

18 Tuesday

A situation you develop blossoms into a meaningful area. It brings a time of pushing back boundaries and challenging set beliefs to increase your life in a unique direction. Moving out of your comfort zone lets you create a journey that offers room to be a game-changer. Implementing proven strategies leads to a shift that provides a pleasing result.

19 Wednesday

You reveal an area that nurtures self-expression and raises creativity in your life. It does bring rising enthusiasm, and this inspiration is your ticket to a successful chapter of growing your life. A lighter and more energetic vibe heightens confidence. It shines a light on connecting with your broader social environment. It brings the green light to pour your energy into achieving a top result. Building stable foundations nurture balance and attract happiness.

20 Thursday ~ Ramadan Ends, New Moon in Taurus 4:12, Hybrid Solar Eclipse, Sun ingress Taurus 8:09, Sun square Pluto 16:26

The Sun square Pluto aspect draws renewal and rejuvenation. Pluto charts a course towards transformation and offers a highly creative part that lights the way forward towards improving your circumstances. The Sun contributes golden beings that offer harmony, transcendence, and rising prospects. This planetary combo elevates creative inclinations due to a New Moon aspect.

21 Friday ~ Mercury turns Retrograde in Taurus at 8:34

Mercury plays havoc with interpersonal bonds and can send communication haywire during its retrograde phase. Buckle up; it's going to be a bumpy ride as your social life goes on a Mercury-driven rollercoaster. If someone's communication triggers an emotional aspect, be mindful that this planetary phase is best with a balanced and understanding approach. Focusing on being flexible will stabilize bonds during this chapter as you navigate forward.

22 Saturday ~ Earth Day, Lyrids Meteor Shower from April 16th -25th

New people enter into your life to expand horizons. It brings a social aspect that highlights a path that draws abundance. Being open to new possibilities brings a pleasing outcome. It offers a fast-moving environment that is stable, progressive, and entertaining. It brings an element of surprise that draws excitement when news arrives that has you thinking about the potential in a new light.

23 Sunday

Life brings new possibilities to light. Your willingness to explore avenues of growth brings new potential flowing into your life. It sparks a big reveal that expands your life outwardly. A promising chapter ahead reshuffle the decks of possibility in your life as you open a gateway forward. A great deal of creativity flows in, sparking significant change. Paying attention to unique options draws a pleasing result.

24 Monday ~ Mercury sextile Mars 3:22

Quick reflexes enable you to spot the diamond in the rough. The Mercury sextile with Mars offers new leads. There is such abundance swirling around the periphery of your life. It is something that continues to tug on your awareness, and this amplifies your intuition. It does direct your attention to a path that opens new possibilities. Following your heart is a journey that is exhilarating and enriching to your spirit.

25 Tuesday ~ Sun sextile Saturn 10:47

Today's sextile brings opportunities that light a path forward. It illuminates fantastic potential that enables you to improve your circumstances. Nurturing your dreams sets the stage to develop your life. It brings a stable foundation that restores the balance. Inner transformation abounds as you set sights on an ambitious goal. You illuminate information needed to plot the chapter ahead.

26 Wednesday

As your priorities change, growing your career becomes a principal focus. You discover a need to put boundaries with people who drain your energy and take a lot of time to deal with in your life. Streamlining and refining your working goals lets you see more benefits as you build security and achieve a successful result. Taking stock enables you to plot the stepping stones to advancement. Growth and stability take shape as rising prospects draw a pleasing outcome.

27 Thursday ~ First Quarter Moon in Leo 21:20

Something new emerges that has you learning the ropes. Finding an unfamiliar environment does let you grow your skills in a new area. It brings a time of change that leads to an awakening. New options arrive that unpack additional opportunities to work with your abilities and refine your talents. It shifts your attention to a clear path that offers a pleasing result for your life.

28 Friday

Something special is ready to bloom in your world. A choice ahead expands the borders of your life. It places you in a solid position to achieve growth. Suppose you have struggled with uncertainty, information along cracks the code to a brighter chapter. It ushers in rising creativity that helps you develop ideas and areas for development. Crafting your plan for future growth draws a pleasing outcome. Life rewards on many levels as you uncover new possibilities.

29 Saturday ~ Mars sextile Uranus 8:04

This sextile brings unique ideas that help you think outside the box to obtain innovative solutions. Uranus places the focus on rebellion, liberation, freedom. It adds a dash of spontaneity into your life today. A surge of new possibilities stirs up a sense of excitement. News reaches you that unlocks a gateway towards future growth. Life is active and busy, letting you initiate developing goals.

30 Sunday

A refreshing change emerges when news arrives that sparks a viable option forward. Being innovative and adaptive helps you push back barriers and create a bridge towards rising prospects in your life. It begins an extended time chasing dreams and unearthing new pathways that offer growth. Acting on instincts takes you further as it taps into your inherent abilities to know the proper path forward for your life. It aligns you with growing your life in a unique direction.

May

Sun	Mon	Tue	Wed	Thu	Fri	Sat
	1	2	3	4	5	6
7	8	9	10	11	12	13
14	15	16	17	18	19	20
21	22	23	24	25	26	27
28	29	30	31			

AQUARIUS
VIRGO TAURUS
SCORPIO STARS
MARS SUN
WEDDING WEALTH FORTUNE
ARIES CAPRICORN CALENDAR
LOVE ASTROLOGY
GEMINI MOON MONTH
HOROSCOPE
LEO
SAGITTARIUS HAPPINESS
BIRTHDAY ASTRONOMY
CANCER LIBRA NEPTUNE DATE ZODIAC
EARTH
PISCES SKY SIGN
TODAY DAILY WEEKLY
CONSTELLATION MONTHLY

NEW MOON

FLOWER MOON

1 Monday ~ Beltane/May Day, Pluto turns retrograde in Aquarius 18:39, Sun conjunct Mercury 23:27

Pluto is the modern ruler of Scorpio; it symbolizes how we experience power, renewal, rebirth, and mysterious or subconscious forces. This retrograde phase lasts until October. It allows you to dive deep and explore inner realms and darker aspects of your personality ordinarily hidden from view. Understanding your psyche on a deeper level provides access to the forces driving your personality. It lets you comprehend the why and wherefore's behind desires.

2 Tuesday

You touch down on a landscape ripe with options. In terms of manifestation, your abilities are growing. It opens a bevy of possibilities that offer growth and progression. You move in a direction that triggers a cascade of exciting potential. It brings the magic coursing into your life as your instincts spot a diamond in the rough. Getting involved with this area puts a shine on your talents.

3 Wednesday

You enter a busy time that brings new possibilities into your life. Generating your own leads fuels creativity, and this brings compelling benefits. As you discover new options, you drift away from outworn areas and embrace the blessings that nurture your life. Fortune favors expansion; it is a time that lightens the load. This new energy sees life progressing forward towards an enriching chapter.

4 Thursday ~ Venus square Neptune 17:40

A Venus square Neptune aspect offers a dreamy quality. It provides the perfect vibe for engaging in the big sky dreaming about your perfect romantic escapade. While fairytales in the sky offer relaxation and escapism, it's important to remember that this dreaminess could lead to delusion if you overly focus on something currently out of reach. Understanding the escapism and creative elements at play enables you to dream big and still feel grounded in reality.

5 Friday ~ Venus sextile Jupiter 4:02, Flower Full Moon in Scorpio 17:34 Penumbral Lunar Eclipse

Venus and Jupiter's sextile create beneficial and harmonious vibrations for your romantic life. Good luck and rising prospects bring warmth and social engagement. Things are shaping up to be an excellent time for personal growth. Life picks up as the pace becomes more active and dynamic. It rules a time of togetherness and harmony.

6 Saturday ~ Eta Aquarids Meteor Shower April 19th - May 28th

A social aspect draws excitement as it is a gateway that opens to a rosy and sunny part. Life becomes brighter as greener pastures beckon and tempt you to engage with your broader circle of friends. News arrives that brings a boost; it lets you nurture your life and head towards an upward trend of rising prospects. You enter a chapter that focuses on creativity, self-expression, and vibrant possibilities. It brings enriching and warm conversations.

7 Sunday ~ Venus ingress Cancer 14:20

Adventure and excitement figure prominently in the chapter ahead. It does see a social environment that connects you with others. It is an expressive, creative, and enriching time. New potential sweeps in with some significant changes in tow. It helps you kick off a path that sees life becoming energizing and active. You can get busy and embrace this social environment as it shines a light on connecting with friends.

8 Monday

Being methodical and working on the task at hand build stable foundations that usher in the terrific potential for your working life. You discover a blossoming journey ahead enables top results. Attention to detail and avoiding distractions brings a top result. You enter a rising aspect in regards to your career path. It does get a positive environment that ushers in a busy time. Productivity shines brightly, and this brings terrific feedback.

9 Tuesday ~ Sun conjunct Uranus 19:55

A positive influence brings a boost which sparks new options. It opens a journey that holds blessings and offers to revolutionize the potential possible in your world. Incoming communication increases potential in your social life. It gets life on track for expansion as you get busy connecting with your broader circle of friends. It shines a light that nurtures thoughtful discussions and mingling with valued companions.

10 Wednesday

Life becomes more settled as you build stability through persevering and refining your skills. You see the marked improvement that offers room to progress your working life. The potential around your career ripens and blossoms into a powerful path forward. You ground yourself in the basics, getting back to building a stable growth phase becomes a priority. As foundations improve, you nurture more balance in your working life.

11 Thursday

Life brings new energy that inspires and delights. It's a fresh chapter of potential. It teams you up with other enterprising people who understand you on a deeper level. Taking your situation to a new level places you in the box seat to advance a lofty goal. It brings you in contact with others who offer support and wisdom. This connected chapter highlights a team approach that draws dividends.

12 Friday ~ Mercury sextile Saturn 8:32, Last Quarter Moon in Aquarius 14:28

Mercury sextile Saturn gives your Friday a boost which helps you tidy up loose ends before the weekend. Mental acuity rises, bringing a focused mind and increased powers of observation lets you see what needs addressing. Today's other cognitive improvements include excellent concentration, good memory, and organization skills. With everything running smoothly in your working life, you can enjoy the weekend ahead knowing you have taken care of business.

13 Saturday ~ Mercury sextile Venus 2:41, Venus trine Saturn 6:56

Mercury sextile Venus offers a social and friendly influence making this a great day to connect with your tribe. Clicking with kindred spirits expands your life and takes you to a suitable landscape to progress your social life. It does bring lively discussions and the sharing of thoughts and ideas. It plants the seeds that, in time, flourish into a beautiful journey.

14 Sunday ~ Mother's Day (US)

This time can feel sentimental as nostalgia makes a grand entrance into your world. It does have your thoughts turning back to a previous chapter. Taking time to integrate and process your situation's changes draws peace and stability. It brings a social environment that puts you in contact with friends and family. It is a happy day that nurtures your spirit and draws abundant sharing with loved ones.

15 Monday ~ Mercury turns direct in Taurus 3:16, Mars trine Neptune 13:44

With Mercury turning direct today, the focus is on your social life. Mars forms a trine with Neptune, enhancing potential as confidence rises and you feel ready for social engagement. It offers the perfect solution for the dodgems as you get busy being self-expressive, communicative, and creative. You enter a phase of growth and expansion that gets a boost to your life. It fuels your motivation, giving you the inspiration needed to overcome barriers and chase your dreams.

16 Tuesday ~ Jupiter ingress Taurus 17:01

As creativity heightens, it brings an epiphany that provides an open road of possibility. Stirring the pot of manifestation brings impressive results to your door. Being available to change brings a time of growth and prosperity that restores equilibrium and gives a more stable basis to the foundations in your life. Peeling back the layers of your ideas lets you get to the root of your vision.

17 Wednesday

A new chapter that has you working on improving security and stability. It offers a firm and robust basis from which to grow your life. A dream is explored and nurtured. This project becomes a vital aspect that releases. Planning and strategy play an important part that takes you towards success. It helps you capitalize on your talents and puts your best qualities in the spotlight.

18 Thursday ~ Jupiter square Pluto 1:09, Sun sextile Neptune 8:59

Today's Jupiter square Pluto brings extra drive and increased energy to complete projects and finish up your to-do list. Neptune also boosts your goals as a sextile with the Sun helps you find the resources and support needed to manifest your vision. You can bring your dreams to reality as the planets have your back today, attracting rising prospects into your life.

19 Friday ~ Mercury sextile Saturn 6:50 New Moon in Taurus 15:54

Today, Mercury, Saturn sextile boosts your communication skills and confidence. Add in a dash of New Moon inspiration and aspiration, and you have the perfect mix for engaging in brainstorming with valued companions. Sharing ideas and adding creative ingredients into the pot of manifestation helps you develop a winning trajectory from which to grow your world next month.

20 Saturday ~ Mars ingress Leo 15:24

Mars lands in Leo, and this raises confidence. It's time to go big and be proud and bold. Your best qualities enter the spotlight and gain recognition soon. It brings a page-turning chapter when the path ahead clears. A strong focus on self-development becomes the catalyst for change. Your efforts to improve your situation reward you with an enterprising approach. It lets you make your mark on a journey that offers room for progression.

21 Sunday ~ Mars opposed Pluto 3:11, Sun ingress Gemini 7:04,
Sun trine Pluto 13:58

Mars connects with a competitive edge today that could see your authority tested. The Sun trine Pluto aspect also adds fuel to the fire as it increases your desire to gain power and feed your ambitious streak. You seek opportunities to elevate your standing among peers and co-workers today. Climbing the ladder towards success becomes a dominant factor.

22 Monday ~ Victoria Day (Canada), Sun sextile Mars 5:56

The Sun sextile Mars transit brings vital energy and renewed zest for life. Your creativity is dynamic and continuously changing, evolving, and growing. It places you in the box seat to take advantage of new possibilities that tempt you forward. You head towards a chapter that emphasizes growth. It sets you correctly to take advantage of an intriguing offer earmarked for your life.

23 Tuesday ~ Mars square Jupiter 5:13

Today's Mars square Jupiter offers a positive influence that increases stamina and boosts your energy. Enthusiasm for the task at hand rises, boosting productivity and enabling you to deal with the day's demands efficiently and capably. Removing the elements that no longer serve your purpose places you on the fast track to improve your circumstances. Being flexible and adaptable to change lets you swivel and circumnavigate complexities easily.

24 Wednesday

A vital life goal comes into focus soon. It lets you get organized and devote yourself to developing a worthwhile area. Focusing on this project without distraction offers valuable results. It polishes your talents and puts a shine on your abilities. It represents a time of enormous personal growth that extends your reach into new areas of interest. It provides a sturdy foundation and structure around your life.

25 Thursday ~ Shavuot (Begins at sunset)

Curious changes ahead shift your focus forward. It brings a pivotal time that launches a fresh cycle of growth. You have a lot going on in your life, bringing new options ripe for progression. It helps you claim your confidence back as you adopt a proactive mindset and develop your dreams. Creativity soars under this powerful positive influence. It brings a new landscape into view.

26 Friday ~ Venus sextile Uranus 7:36

Today's sextile promotes a vibrant and active social life. With Venus charming and Uranus adding a dash of spontaneity to your weekend plans, it assures a fun and lively time shared with friends. You focus your energy on bonds that offer personal growth and abundance. It brings an enchanting time that casts a spell on your life. It lets you schedule activities that are fun and lively.

27 Saturday ~ Shavuot (Ends at sunset), First Quarter Moon in Virgo 15:22

A social aspect ahead helps open your life to new people and possibilities. It brings a cycle of good fortune that kicks off a chapter of progressing your social life. It highlights a new companion who enters your life with wisdom and grace. It brings a productive and adventurous time where significant change is possible. Improving your circumstances is a theme that resonates soundly over the coming weeks.

28 Sunday

Favorable changes are coming up. It kicks off a social environment that beckons you to expand your horizons. It brings a more active environment that shifts your focus towards mingling and networking. Life stabilizes, and you enjoy smooth sailing as new possibilities emerge. Information arrives that opens a path worth growing. An emphasis on improving circumstances draws a pleasing result.

JUNE

Sun	Mon	Tue	Wed	Thu	Fri	Sat
				1	2	3
4	5	6	7	8	9	10
11	12	13	14	15	16	17
18	19	20	21	22	23	24
25	26	27	28	29	30	

NEW MOON

STRAWBERRY MOON

29 Monday ~ Memorial Day, Mercury at Greatest Elongation 24.9W

The future is looking rosy as it brings new options to your door. A focus on self-development and growth provides pathways forward. It supports movement, discovery, and rising prospects. You weave pure magic by tapping into innovative options. It lets you chart a course towards a journey that fans the flames of your inspiration with new ideas and endeavors.

30 Tuesday

Changes ahead bring light energy into your working life. It helps get a boost that draws heightened motivation and enthusiasm to the task at hand. You complete assignments and projects promptly. Streamlining the path ahead puts you at an advantage; it brings the news of a promotion in the pipeline. A step up to a new area of interest brings an energizing time of extending your reach into new areas.

31 Wednesday

Progression ahead underscores a time of change and discovery. You unearth new leads, and this offers expansion and growth. Indeed, opening the path brings a blossoming chapter of working with your abilities and growing your skills. Prospects burn brightly as new offers help you scope out a new pathway towards success. A vital transition ahead restores and rejuvenates; it brings good news to your door.

1 Thursday

News arrives that is worth its weight in gold. It brings support that is a welcome boost. It ushers in possibilities for your social life that are life-affirming and enriching. It helps you move in a positive direction as you scope out a journey that speaks volumes to the person you are becoming. Confidence heightens, enabling you to make the snap decisions that grow your world.

2 Friday ~ Venus trine Neptune 22:42

Creativity and imagination are peaking under the blissful Venus, Neptune trine. Harmony, equilibrium, and well-being soar under this positive influence. Self-expression is rising, cultivating a unique path that captures the essence of artistic inclinations. Venus showers positivity over your social life, improving personal bonds. It kickstarts beautiful potential that brings opportunities to socialize and network in your wider community.

3 Saturday

You may be feeling restless; a change of scene is therapeutic and beneficial for your spirit. It brings a time that offers new options to explore. It helps you push back boundaries and make strides on improving your life. A fascinating opportunity creates a stir of interest, motivating to unearth progress. Finally, you arrive at a gateway that offers a new chapter of potential.

4 Sunday ~ Strawberry Full Moon in Sagittarius 3:42,
Mercury conjunct Uranus 19:50

Mercury and Uranus form a positive aspect that heightens mental abilities. Increasing mental stimulation promotes fresh ideas in your life today. Technology, messages, and communication all play a part in sparking inspiration and fostering possibilities for future development. It leads to discussing future projects and endeavors with a kindred spirit.

5 Monday ~ Venus ingress Leo 13:42, Venus opposed Pluto 16:04

News ahead lets you chart a course towards developing dreams. It brings a time when you focus on planning larger goals. It enables you to progress forward and take a path that aligns with the person you are becoming. It brings expansive options that let you dive into new territory. Opening the book on a new chapter heightens creativity; it focuses on using your abilities to establish an enterprising journey ahead.

6 Tuesday

Complexities soon shift as a new landscape takes shape. Your willingness to open up to new people and possibilities brings potential flowing into your world. It is an inspiring time that shines a light on nurturing dreams and chasing inspiration. A lucky aspect ahead draws good fortune and harmony into your life. It heightens creativity and brings expansion to your table when you unearth a lead worth developing.

7 Wednesday

The work you undertake is well received and appreciated by those who count. It draws a path that moves you in alignment with progressing your career path forward. Setting barriers with people who incite drama draws more balance into your working life. Focusing on your area brings a productive phase of growing the potential possible. It lands you in an environment that offers progression.

8 Thursday

Researching and strategizing helps plot a course towards a pleasing result. It triggers a journey that grows your skills and nurtures your abilities. It culminates in an active and productive chapter that brings a boost into your life. Inspiration and creativity are rising, creating a potent brew of manifestation at your disposal. Exploring the possibilities kicks off a chapter of growth and prosperity, planning future goals and seeing their development through completion.

9 Friday

Setting intentions lights a clear path that helps manifest your vision in due course. However, life reveals a curious twist when you reveal secret news and the way ahead clears. It brings the developments that offer progression and joy. It brings a new perspective and lets you nurture bonds through expansive conversations. Further information arrives that leads to a soul-stirring time of discovery and adventure.

10 Saturday ~ Last Quarter Moon in Pisces 19:31

A carefree and happy time is ahead for your life. You enter a time of increasing possibilities; it brings something special into your world. It draws an energizing chapter that lights a path towards a brighter environment. It captures the essence of your imagination as it takes you to a radiant time that offers the gift of self-expression and heightened creativity. It brings new options to your table that draw excitement.

11 Sunday ~ Mercury ingress Gemini 10:24, Mercury trine Pluto 10:27, Pluto ingress Capricorn 13:12, Venus square Jupiter 15:39

Today's Venus square Jupiter planetary alignment offers good things for your social life. It is the perfect time to engage with friends; lively discussions nurture creativity. It is a prime time for letting your hair down and having fun in a relaxing environment that draws stability into your world. You enter a time where you become more expressive about your needs and goals.

12 Monday

News arrives, and it's best to make a firm decision. Committing to a course of action brings a path that offers abundance. Everything turns out for the best. Sometimes the most remarkable growth occurs when you extend your reach into new areas. As you teeter on the precipice of change, harnessing your inner strength of spirit helps you expand horizons while maintaining a stable basis. Sound foundations draw stability, security, and balance.

13 Tuesday

Life is ripe with potential ready to blossom. It brings fresh ideas that let you see the path ahead clearly. You reveal a landscape of exciting options that draw a purposeful and innovative journey towards an active and productive environment. It lets you make progress around some of your larger goals. Chasing your dreams is a vital priority and takes you towards embracing a growth path.

14 Wednesday ~ Flag Day

You are in a time of change that has the power to sweep away negativity. It releases blocks and removes limitations that have held you back. It places you in the correct alignment to draw new possibilities. It grows ambitions and adds fuel to your inspiration. You uncover information that brings a boost to your spirit. It creates a bridge towards a brighter chapter and marks the start of something big arriving in your world.

15 Thursday

You get involved with a venture that goes exceedingly well, and this jumpstarts further opportunities ahead. It lets you make notable tracks on improving your circumstances. An insightful person shares advice, which brings an opportunity for collaboration that sparks an enterprising time. It draws an active and productive chapter of working with your abilities and growing a vision for future growth.

16 Friday

You are ready to break free of limitations and expand your life into new areas. Indeed, an invitation ahead offers a social aspect that is reinvigorating. Suddenly, the path ahead clears. It brings a succession of events culminating in an enriching chapter shared with friends. It sets the scene for a social environment that has you mingling with kindred spirits. It places you in the box seat to form new friends and widen your social circle.

17 Saturday ~ Saturn turns Retrograde in Pisces 16:52

Saturn is a planet that rules boundaries, structure, and discipline. This retrograde draws balance and righteousness into your situation. Making fair and reasonable choices and decisions connects with karma to achieve a fair and beneficial outcome. You may be about to face a decision in your life. Facing the truth of a situation shines a light on where the scales may be tipped unevenly to one side, creating a sense of imbalance in your life.

18 Sunday ~ New Moon in Cancer 4:38, Father's Day (US)

Positive change ahead brings goodness to the top of your world. It unearths new possibilities for your social life. It brings opportunities to develop a more prosperous home and family life. The seeds you plant mark a new beginning. It triggers an original path that heightens creativity and lets you plan future dreams and goals. It helps you see your life from a unique perspective that is heartening.

19 Monday ~ Sun square Neptune 3:53, Jupiter sextile Saturn 15:53

Today, the Neptune square Sun aspect can water down your ambitions, leaving you feeling foggy and indecisive. If your vision feels clouded, going back over your plans can help make sure they continue to align with your vision for future growth. Recommitting to developing your career goals can help shift some of the clouds that hang over your working life today. If the boss gives you a hard time, blame it on Neptune for bringing Monday woes into your working life.

20 Tuesday

Changes ahead keep you on your toes. It transitions you towards a new chapter, and in doing so, you leave outworn aspects of the past behind. It sees motivation returning full force. Life takes on a rosy hue as you create a path that draws abundance. An attractive possibility makes itself known, and it is a powerful lure that takes you out of your comfort zone. It rekindles your vitality and has you feeling motivated to expand your horizons.

21 Wednesday ~ Midsummer/Litha Solstice 14:58, Mercury sextile Mars 15:23

The Mercury sextile Mars aspect today fosters joint projects and cooperation. Getting involved with a group endeavor stimulates your mind and brings new possibilities. Brainstorming sessions offer a trailblazing path towards innovative solutions and rising prospects. Joining forces and strategizing with like-minded people cultivate an excellent success rate. It helps you cover the bases by blending other people's talents into the mix of potential at your disposal.

22 Thursday

A busy aspect ahead brings new potential into your social life. It helps you create the stepping stone towards new goals which draw security and harmony into your surroundings. A time of discovery overhead connects you with someone who offers insight and guidance. It triggers an active phase of sharing conversations and enjoying life. A long-forgotten dream makes a grand entrance into your life soon.

23 Friday

You have a golden touch for anything you turn your hand to at this time. It draws a pleasing outcome is that gets you on track to expand horizons into new areas. Struggles fade away as a brilliant aspect arrives to tempt you forward. It offers a social path and a chance for collaboration with a kindred spirit. Sharing thoughts and ideas light a creative and artistic aspect that heightens innovative thinking. Brainstorming cracks the code to expand the potential in your life.

24 Saturday

You can expect a few twists and turns as you reveal a surprise. It opens a chapter of discovery that lets you build a bridge towards a brighter future. You invest your time in developing an area that shows promise. It brings a project that becomes a jewel in your crown. The potential for success moves forward in leaps and bounds. It links up to positive change that draws blessings in your world. It helps you evaluate goals and lets you figure out new areas of growth.

25 Sunday

Surprise news brings tremendous changes to your home life. You move forward with a clear head that enables progress to occur. Taking care of business, you soon get cracking on developing your vision. Honing in on your true purpose marks a necessary time of transition that sees elevated potential flowing into your world. Using the energy of manifestation lets you fast-track a cycle of growth.

26 Monday ~ First Quarter Moon in Libra 7:50, Mars square Uranus 9:22

There may be an influence around your energy that blocks progress. Taking a moment to gain insight into the different areas that pull your time gives you insight into where to focus best to move forward. Life gets a boost when news arrives that sparks new options worth your consideration. It opens a path that holds blessings and offers a journey to grow your life.

27 Tuesday ~ Mercury ingress Cancer 12:22

Your curiosity uncovers fantastic potential ahead. Investigating options draws valuable rewards. It helps you shift gears and forge a path towards your dreams. It connects you with a pathway of learning and growth. It takes your abilities towards advancement, and this draws a productive environment that sees you working smarter, not harder. Your prospects are rising. It opens the door to an active and productive environment that helps expand into new directions.

28 Wednesday

You make notable tracks on improving your situation. A transition ahead shines a light on a viable path that helps you move forward. It brings a grounded time that keeps life progressing towards new options. It brings positive momentum that extends your reach into an area worth growing. After some soul-searching, you get involved with developing your skills, refining your talents draws expanding options.

29 Thursday ~ Sun trine Saturn 1:42

Today's Sun trine Saturn offers constructive dialogues and thoughtful ideas that enhance your creativity and stimulate new pathways of possibility in your life. A positive influence nurtures unique approaches that capitalize on the potential possible in your surroundings. It kicks off a chapter of sunshine and sparkle. As you continue to develop your ideas, your creativity takes you places. Abilities spread like wildfire as you explore a journey of growth that nourishes your spirit.

July

Sun	Mon	Tue	Wed	Thu	Fri	Sat
						1
2	3	4	5	6	7	8
9	10	11	12	13	14	15
16	17	18	19	20	21	22
23	24	25	26	27	28	29
30	31					

New Moon

BUCK MOON

30 Friday ~ Neptune turns Retrograde in Pisces, 19:28

Neptune retrograde strips away delusions, allusions, and fanciful thinking. Under the glare of more informed thought processes, you build tangible growth pathways to take your talents to the next level. This phase enables you to sink your teeth in developing goals that offer fruitful results. Moving away from areas that have clouded your thinking and brought doubt to your judgment does provide you with clear stepping stones that take you towards success.

1 Saturday ~ Canada Day, Sun conjunct Mercury 5:05, Mercury sextile Jupiter 7:10, Sun sextile Jupiter 10:26

Open-mindedness, curiosity, and a quest for adventure are prominent aspects as a Mercury sextile Jupiter alignment fosters creativity and self-expression. This transit favors organization, planning, and the development of longer-term goals. Reviewing plans and streamlining your vision enables you to cut to the chase and find a practical path to progress your goals. New information emerges to catch your interest and spur you to advance your life.

2 Sunday ~ Venus square Uranus 14:32

An increased need for freedom and liberation can destabilize as Venus faces Uranus in a square alignment. Being mindful of balancing interpersonal bonds while being self-expressive and creative can ease tensions. At the same time, you can let your hair down and enjoy a freedom-driven chapter of fun and excitement. It does bring a new endeavor that gets you involved with a project that inspires your mind.

3 Monday ~ Super Moon, Buck Full Moon in Capricorn 11:40

Letting go of past baggage and releasing sensitive feelings helps shut the door on a problematic area that is best left behind. Feeling nostalgic can be part of this process as it lets you remove outworn regions by bringing them to the surface. It takes you towards healing and creates space for unique opportunities to emerge in your life. A necessary transition facilitates moving forward towards a happier phase.

4 Tuesday ~ Independence Day

Today brings harmony into focus as it connects you with a broader social environment that supports well-being and abundance. A situation you nurture blossoms into a powerful journey forward for your life. It brings an extraordinary time that releases heaviness and brings joy flowing into your world. It helps you reawaken to the vibrant landscape of potential that surrounds your life.

5 Wednesday

Exploring options lets life back on track as you discover a pathway that draws transformation. It brings sweeping changes you can embrace as part of your evolution. Your willingness to seek solutions brings new opportunities. Rearranging and streamlining the path ahead helps open this exciting avenue that lets you turn a corner and head towards growth. A desire to branch out and learn new areas adds to your skills and abilities.

6 Thursday

A change of scene is on the horizon. It hits the ticket for a happy chapter of re-establishing foundations. It reboots the potential possible in your life. It brings good fortune and prosperity, and this lighter energy flow nurtures your inspiration and rejuvenates your spirit. It shifts your situation forward to a more grounded and balanced environment. It rules a time of increasing abundance that offers harmony and well-being.

7 Friday

News ahead brings an influx of opportunities that shine a light on expanding your world. It brings a new direction that offers growth, learning, and stability. At the crux of this active progression phase, you discover a new adventure that shows the sweet taste of success. Under this influence, you can reach for more prosperity as you advance your skills and engage with the dance of life. It lets you establish a positive shift to your life and work balance.

8 Saturday

You have recently undergone many changes, which can leave your foundations feeling shaky. Immersing yourself in building the basics of life, you ground your energy in an area that offers room to grow your situation. It creates a balanced and stable environment to move forward and towards growth. A curious change looms overhead, bringing a calming influence into your life. It radiates abundance and tranquillity, bringing fullness and harmony into view.

9 Sunday ~ Mercury trine Neptune 23:56

Mercury in trine with Neptune focuses on your dreams and goals; it adds mental clarity that helps you stay focused as you work towards realizing your vision. Something you hope to reach in your life can reach fruition with the correct planning, adjustments, and focus. Creating space to nurture your priorities lets you reap the rewards of a dedicated approach that offers an increasing success rate.

10 Monday ~ Last Quarter Moon in Aries 1:48, Mars ingress Virgo 11:34, Mercury opposed Pluto 20:47

A shift ahead brings adventure and excitement into your world. It helps you break free of limitations and expand your life into a new area. Information arrives that leads to exciting ideas and goals taking shape. It enables you to push ahead towards your vision as it shines the spotlight on a path worth growing. Life brings a positive influence into your surroundings.

11 Tuesday ~ Mercury ingress Leo 4:09

A new role on offer shifts your focus towards a grounded chapter of developing your working life. It tempts you forward towards a time of fast growth. Moving to an abundant mindset draws rewards. You get busy in an active and dynamic environment, which kickstarts a change journey. Rising prospects ahead offer you a bevy of potential career paths to explore. You mark a significant turning point that culminates in the room to progress your career path.

12 Wednesday

News arrives in a blaze of glory. It comes out of the blue, so you may need some time to assimilate this information and get a handle on what it means for your life. But, it lets you chart a strong path towards growth and progression. Happy news provides a fresh start that lights your life with new opportunities. It enables you to direct your energy towards interests that hold meaning for your life. It brings stabilizing and supportive energy that gives a sense of security.

13 Thursday

You can optimize your life by exploring all avenues of growth. It activates a driven chapter that brings the ideal conditions to work with your creativity and create a shift forward. It draws an abundant journey of possibilities and magic. You make steady progress towards advancing your talents into a new area. As you launch towards developing a vision, you connect with kindred spirits who support and offer guidance.

14 Friday ~ Sun sextile Uranus 23:02

In sextile with the Sun, Uranus captures the essence of surprises, new information, and discoveries. Something new and exciting is ready to manifest in your life. Being open to new people and possibilities charts a course towards rising prospects. Exploring your more unique environment brings freedom and expansion. It has you in the mood to seek out adventure and connect with impromptu opportunities to mingle.

15 Saturday

Changes ahead, put developing your dreams on the front burner. It ignites inspiration, sparking a trailblazing time of growing your world. A time of transformation heats a lighter chapter that offers social engagement and community involvement. It launches a time of promoting stable foundations as you get busy with new projects and endeavors on the home front. An insightful person opens the door to a bright chapter ahead.

16 Sunday

A prominent aspect comes into view. It brings an emphasis on your home life which builds more secure foundations. Adopting a gentle approach offers a pleasing result as it nurtures a balanced path forward. It places your vision towards developing growth and happiness. It brings a transformation that provides to reshuffle the decks of potential in your life. Your awareness guides this process as you open the door to a fresh start in your life.

17 Monday ~ Mercury square Jupiter 12:48, New Moon in Cancer 18:32

You enter a busy time that offers advancement. It provides a glorious aspect that draws security and prosperity into your life. Advancing your job is a positive sign that reassures you that you are heading in the right direction. Your status continues to rise in your industry, bringing improvement into your world. Life becomes lighter and sweeter as you step out towards breaking new ground. Little breaks the stride as you enter an enterprising chapter ahead.

18 Tuesday ~ Islamic New Year

The future gets you to develop your abilities and expand your skillset into new areas. Amplifying your talents nurtures creativity. It brings a high note into your life that sets the tone for developing new goals and progression areas. You can create headway on achieving further growth by expanding horizons and pushing back boundaries that limit progress. It connects you to a path that draws learning, which helps you make the most of your talents.

19 Wednesday

Information arrives soon that sparks your attention. It brings a fertile ground to tackle your dreams and explore new options that advance your vision forward. It brings the magic of possibility into your life, and this whets your appetite as it gets a sweet taste of success. It lets you sink your teeth into developing an ambitious project—creating a funnel for your excess energy channels your abilities into an exciting area.

20 Thursday ~ Sun trine Neptune 13:06, Mars opposed Saturn 20:39

The Sun trine Neptune alignment raises the vibration around your life. It focuses on improving the circumstances in your life and helping others who face difficult circumstances. Creativity is a valuable resource that lets you craft plans that offer tangible impacts that enhance your world. Developing your vision draws rewards and prosperity. A richer life experience emerges and brings peace into your world.

21 Friday

A time of abundance and magic is looming. You head towards a chapter that glimmers with potential. Listening to your intuition holds you in the highest alignment to grow your life and achieve a fantastic outcome. You soon tap into a path of promise that continues a more comprehensive theme of expanding horizons occurring in your life.

22 Saturday ~ Sun opposed Pluto 3:52

The Sun shines a light on a hidden aspect Pluto keeps out of sight in your day-to-day life. This opposition Pluto creates a doorway through which pockets of the inner self, spirit, and primal energy can reach the surface of your awareness. It shines a light on subconscious desires and instincts. Life has an edgier aspect that can feel unsettling today. It does get you in touch with hidden depths that spark an internal dialogue as you reveal a personal element of your personality.

23 Sunday ~ Venus turns Retrograde in Leo 1:33, Sun ingress Leo 1:47

Venus turns retrograde, which slows the progress down around your love life. Romantic development slows down or stagnates during this phase. Focus on the building blocks as the journey is as important as the final destination. Taking time to pause and reflect on your life's journey grounds your foundations and brings more balance into your environment. You can utilize the pearls of wisdom gathered from past lessons to shift gears and adopt a winning approach.

24 Monday

New ideas and information bring a burst of inspiration flowing into your world that reinvigorates your foundations from the ground up. It gets a chance to use your abilities and grow your talents into new areas. It offers a unique learning experience and brings rising prospects. Seeing the moves of others brings the benefit of secret knowledge that enables you to navigate the path adeptly. It does move you out of your comfort zone, but this is where the growth occurs.

25 Tuesday ~ First Quarter Moon in Libra 22:06

Focusing on growing your abilities and working with your talents triggers an enterprising path ahead. It lets you forge a firm basis from which to extend your life outwardly. Confidence rises, and this takes your abilities to a new level. Advancement is imminent, which lets you see a brighter picture of possible possibilities when expanding horizons. Focusing on strategy with friends draws a trailblazing chapter of exploring new options.

26 Wednesday

Life takes on a lighter hue, and under this influence, you transform potential. It jumpstarts a new area that sparks positive growth. It draws a highly productive cycle that is active and social. It connects you to a happy chapter that sees you circulating with friends. It brings lively discussions and dynamic conversations that spark new possibilities. Chasing leads generates new options that inspire change. Surprise news ahead shifts your focus forward to new endeavors.

27 Thursday ~ Mercury conjunct Venus 15:15

The Mercury conjunct Venus aspect today bodes well for your personal life. Communication flows, as does feelings, emotions, and sentiments. The time is right to share loving thoughts and receive positive feedback from someone who holds meaning in your life. You let your hair down and communicate openly. It brings a sense of support and connection that draws enrichment.

28 Friday ~ Delta Aquarids Meteor Shower. July 12th – August 23rd,
Mercury ingress Virgo 21:29

You are working with your creativity on a course that grows your life. It unleashes your talents and offers your abilities to a broader audience. Shaking off the heavy vibes that have clung to your energy over recent times paves the way forward towards expanding horizons. Listening to the voice within your spirit draws dividends as you move in alignment towards a lofty goal.

29 Saturday

You link up with your broader community environment, which generates a busy time that offers growth for your personal life. It does bring a refreshing change of pace that lets old challenges melt away. It releases the heaviness and brings a path of social growth that nurtures companionship. It offers a positive aspect that draws well-being and harmony into your world. It lifts the lid on a chapter that enriches your life.

30 Sunday

Prioritizing your needs supports well-being; it creates a stable foundation from which to expand your world outwardly. You head towards a time of potential that takes your life in a curious new direction. You begin to see the outline of a journey that offers abundance as inspiration comes flowing into your world to inspire change. Creativity heightens, visionary ideas spark new possibilities. It lets you set sail towards advancing your life into new areas.

AUGUST

Sun	Mon	Tue	Wed	Thu	Fri	Sat
		1	2	3	4	5
6	7	8	9	10	11	12
13	14	15	16	17	18	19
20	21	22	23	24	25	26
27	28	29	30	31		

NEW MOON

STURGEON MOON

31 Monday

A new area ahead widens the borders of your life. It highlights a lively chapter that offers light and playful energy with a side of social engagement. It opens a path towards new adventures. It brings a compelling journey that draws remarkable results. A change of direction ahead opens the floodgates to an enterprising chapter that sets the tone for growing your world. It is a changing environment that lights up new pathways of growth.

1 Tuesday ~ Lammas/Lughnasadh, Super Moon,
Sturgeon Full Moon in Aquarius 18:32, Mars trine Jupiter 20:44

Moving towards greener pastures helps you move away from situations that limit potential. It brings new possibilities into your life. It provides a chance to nurture friendships and draw enrichment into your social life. Lively discussions get insightful ideas and the opportunity to spend more time with your crew of friends. Connecting with your broader circle brings companionship.

2 Wednesday ~ Mercury opposed Saturn 2:16

As Mercury opposes Saturn, it brings heavy vibes into your life. The air of tension leaves a palpable sense of negativity around conversations and communication today. A serious-minded person may seek to have a strongly worded conversation with you. Setting boundaries creating space to nurture the foundations in your life helps restore balance if talks become pessimistic today. Pushing business decisions off for another day is advisable.

3 Thursday

Trying your luck at new enterprises lets you take that extra push towards growing your situation. Forging ahead rewards you with a pleasing outcome. It draws good fortune into your world and sets the stage to raise a path that offers life-changing possibilities. It brings a transition that provides growth and prosperity. Investing your time wisely into developing pertinent goals brings a high degree of change to your table.

4 Friday

Unexpected opportunities provide a chance to grow your skills. a project crops up that offers more range and depth for your creativity. It provides impressive results that advance your skills as it gives you a chance to grow and gain valuable experience. Newfound power propels you forward towards developing your vision. Making the most of this forward momentum helps you manifest your plans.

5 Saturday

Keeping open to meeting people helps cultivate rising prospects. It promotes confidence and enables you to step into a new chapter that initiates growth around your life. Connecting with a lively environment that adds momentum to your goals provides plenty of motivation to expand and grow in a new direction. Dazzling potential tempts you out of your comfort zone, placing you in a stronger position to enhance your social life.

6 Sunday

A positive influence offers expansion and gain, which improves the security in your life. It shifts your emphasis to increasing your life in a direction that promotes a pleasing result. Continuing to engage in developing your abilities heightens artistic expression. A rich landscape of possibility reawakens your senses as new options help you craft a significant journey forward.

7 Monday ~ Sun square Jupiter 12:03

Today's Sun square Jupiter aspect raises confidence and brings good fortune swirling around your life. It does boost your ego, which could lead to you overstepping the mark. Knowing your capabilities and working within the systems you have in place for your life will help keep things in check during this energetic time.

8 Tuesday ~ Last Quarter Moon in Taurus 10:48

You benefit from events on the horizon as a new page opens in your book of life. New possibilities dial down stress levels and leave you feeling inspired. It brings opportunities and experiences that open the door to a brighter future. Indeed, you are undergoing a transition that culminates in a pathway that nurtures well-being and draws abundance into your surroundings. Setting positive intentions creates a positive mindset that keeps you focused forward.

9 Wednesday ~ Venus square Uranus 11:09

A surprise element adds a sense of uncertainty to your personal/social life due to the Venus square Uranus aspect today. It draws freedom and change as you expand your horizons outwardly and embrace a sense of connection with your broader circle of friends. Like-minded people offer engaging discussions and dynamic advice. A new cycle arrives in your life, bringing a welcome boost of invitations that inspire personal growth.

10 Thursday ~ Mercury at Greatest Elongation 27.4 E, Mercury trine Jupiter 12:45

Mercury trine Jupiter today brings a boost into your life. Jupiter is the planet of good luck and fortuitous happenings, which improves the potential possible around your circumstances. An opportunity arrives that sets the stage for new ideas to flourish. It offers an excellent ripple effect that outwardly expands your life. It brings a lucky break that helps you launch into a journey that inspires and motivates growth.

11 Friday

A lovely trend ahead promotes expansion in your life. It brings a chance to work with your creativity and move towards rising prospects. It brings a sense of hope and optimism that surges in your world with new projects and activities on the horizon. Finding a greater understanding of purpose cracks the code to an enterprising time working with your abilities. The possibilities will be plentiful as new options spark growth.

12 Saturday ~ Perseids Meteor Shower July 17th - Aug 24th

Information ahead initiates change as it brings a busy time that gets you in touch with your broader circle of friends. Creativity rises as momentum picks up steam in your social life. It promotes networking with kindred spirits, and this cultivates well-being and happiness. Discussions and decisions ahead focus on growing your life as you connect with friends and explore incoming social opportunities.

13 Sunday

Life becomes more balanced as you lay the groundwork for a stable and secure home environment. Deepening a friendship stimulates your mind and encourages an optimistic outlook. It has you feeling lighter and ready to step out and enjoy a more supportive environment. It brings a time that feels tailor-made for sharing thoughtful discussions.

14 Monday

Movement is imminent around your career path. Life offers new learning opportunities that help grow your working life. A fast-paced environment cracks the code to rising prospects in your career. You discover a new role that offers an enterprising and progressive element. As you explore new leads, you take action towards growing your abilities. Your discipline and commitment draw valuable rewards.

15 Tuesday

An idea you begin developing blossoms into a meaningful venture. It brings a chance to work with your abilities and design a path that cultivates your talents. Expanding your life increases optimism as you get busy reshaping goals. You soon come up with viable options worth your time. Investing in your skills brings ample time to explore new interests. It turns the leaf on a chapter that brings happiness and growth.

**16 Wednesday ~ Sun square Uranus 2:34, New Moon in Leo 09:37,
Mars trine Uranus 13:53**

Uranus steals the show today, and you can expect a spontaneous and expressive environment that offers a breath of fresh air in your life. A brighter world of opportunity is ready to emerge in your life. You reveal an exciting avenue that offers a curious sideline for your creative inspiration. Unleashing your skills in a broader arena of potential brings opportunities to grow your talents.

17 Thursday

Something new on offer rewards you with a positive influence. It opens the door to a brighter chapter that grows your life in a meaningful area. It brings lighter energy into your life, which helps shore up any flagging foundations. It offers a prime time to set new goals and plan the path. Reaching for your dreams directs your energy towards growing your life and expanding horizons which promote happiness.

18 Friday

Fantastic news ahead brings a refreshing option. Pursuing your dreams advances life forward in an exciting fashion. It places you in a favorable alignment to create growth as you head towards higher prospects. Stimulating new leads bolsters confidence and harnesses the energy of optimism to achieve stellar results. It brings a social aspect and a chance to circulate with your broader circle of friends.

19 Saturday

Life brings faster as change and opportunity emerge and align you with growing your circumstances. Striking while the iron is hot helps put plans into action. You receive an important message that offers a missing puzzle piece. It leads to a meaningful conversation that lets you learn more about an area that had felt incomplete. Clearing out outworn energy provides a refreshing landscape that lets you move forward with growth plans.

20 Sunday

Doing some soul-searching around sensitive areas will provide clarity into the path ahead. A sentimental theme carries your thoughts back to the past; it does see life come full circle, enabling you to shut the door on an area that feels complete. Taking time to build stable foundations in your life draws a pleasing result. It draws happiness and harmony into your world as you get involved with nurturing your life.

21 Monday

A new influence arrives in your life. It brings opportunities to collaborate and get involved in developing a group opportunity. Giving teamwork a try draws expansion into your life. It gives you a road that nurtures your abilities and grows your talents. It draws supportive and lively ideas that initiate new plans and endeavors. It lets you steadily enhance your foundations as you turn a corner and head towards growth.

22 Tuesday ~ Venus square Jupiter 12:13, Mars opposed Neptune 20:33

A Venus Jupiter square offers rising prospects for your love life. You will have trouble concentrating on the task at hand as fun moments capture your attention. It lets you chart a course towards sharing an enriching chapter with friends and companions. It brings a highly productive cycle that offers a chance to socialize and mingle. As you surround yourself with lighter energy, you draw robust stability that improves the building blocks of your life.

23 Wednesday ~ Sun ingress Virgo 8:58, Mercury turns retrograde 19:59

Mercury turns retrograde and puts a damper on the potential possible in your social life. It can cause miscommunication and issues in your love life. Mercury in retrograde adds an element that turns communication haywire. It disrupts the positive flow of energy in your life. Delay signing contracts or committing to business deals during a retrograde phase. It is an appropriate time for planning, but launch new endeavors after the retrograde cycle completes.

24 Thursday ~ First Quarter Moon in Sagittarius 9:57

Weighing up the path before committing to a decision can help you make informed choices. You gather all the information before committing to a course of action. Not everything that tempts you is in your greatest good. If someone appears too good to be true, it's wise to re-evaluate and be discerning. Setting the bar higher draws the correct path; it takes you on a journey that provides a sunny aspect.

25 Friday ~ Mars trine Pluto 12:22

Today's aspect offers rising prospects for your career. It brings a goal-orientated, disciplined, and centered focus. You round a corner and reach increasing opportunities that bring the right progression conditions. It initiates a time of rapid growth and change that has you feeling excited about the potential possible. It brings something new on offer ushers in nurturing your abilities and advancing your skills.

26 Saturday

Life moves from strength to strength as you nurture your social life. It highlights a time of freedom and adventure that strongly emphasizes promoting personal bonds. As you dissolve the barriers, you take advantage of opportunities to mingle and invitations to share with your broader circle of friends. It ushers in an expressive aspect that cultivates lively discussions, social engagement, and happiness.

27 Sunday ~ Sun opposed Saturn 8:28, Mars ingress Libra r 13:15

A healing influence washes away outworn areas, nourishing your spirit, and opening life to a new start. It represents the light at the end of the tunnel. It describes joy, happiness, and harmony. Things will come together and agree with your path and aid forward movements into something more significant. It reflects contentment, vitality, and self-confidence. It brings rising options that trigger emotional warmth and happiness into your life.

28 Monday

You are close to reaching your goals. Persevering and developing the path ahead reveals a pleasing result for your personal life. Being conscious of proactively expanding boundaries helps crack the code to achieving growth. Working with your strengths gathers a natural momentum that spurs you to achieve your dreams. Life grows in unique ways that seal the deal on a brighter chapter.

29 Tuesday ~ Uranus turns Retrograde in Taurus 2:11

Uranus moving into a retrograde phase boosts idealism; it offers big sky pictures that help motivate change to improve the world around you. This planetary cycle will boost your confidence and foster leadership qualities. It deepens initiative and offers a fresh wind that spurs creativity and an uptick of potential. You amplify the potential by developing solutions that propel you towards greener pastures by using your creative side.

30 Wednesday

Today offers more extensive changes for your life that connects with your higher purpose. It brings expansion, balance, and growth to help expand your horizons. You find the sweet spot in your life that is the key to unlocking new possibilities. Your sense of adventure reawakens to a rich landscape of potential surrounding your life. You are on a journey imbued with opportunity and excitement.

31 Thursday ~ Super Moon, Blue Full Moon in Pisces 1:36

A time of contemplation draws clarity into the path ahead. It helps you sweep away the outworn areas that hold no future benefits. Changes become the building blocks to a new chapter of life. It expands horizons and helps you invest your energy into upgrading your life. It points you towards a journey of working with your talents and developing career options. Advancing life towards new areas facilitates growth as you grow your skills in a unique direction.

SEPTEMBER

Sun	Mon	Tue	Wed	Thu	Fri	Sat
					1	2
3	4	5	6	7	8	9
10	11	12	13	14	15	16
17	18	19	20	21	22	23
24	25	26	27	28	29	30

wild
SOUL

NEW MOON

CORN/HARVEST MOON

1 Friday

Growth occurs in both your career and social life. Networking draws a pleasing result as you discover new companions worth your time. It opens the door to a more connected environment that spells magic around your life. As an insightful cast of characters enters your social life, you reveal collaboration and joint venture opportunities. A more active and productive pace offers a turning point that leads to growth.

2 Saturday

You lift the lid on an enterprising chapter when unexpected news delivers fresh potential. It gives you the green light to shift your focus towards developing an area of interest that offers a nugget of gold. Nurturing this path draws a meaningful environment that lets you take advantage of a social aspect. Abundance is a theme that resonates strongly around your surroundings during this vital time.

3 Sunday

News arrives that draws an adventurous time of liberation, freedom, and expansion. It offers an opportunity to socialize that connects you with a broader world of potential. Nurturing friendships draw enriching options to light that offer lively discussions and engaging company. Life takes a surprising turn, prompting you to become more proactive about expanding your world outwardly. It clears the path towards developing a new enterprise.

4 Monday ~ Labor Day, Venus turns direct in Leo 1:19,
Mercury trine Jupiter 10:29, Jupiter turns Retrograde in Taurus 14:14

Venus turns direct and brings an open road of potential into your love life. It lets you schedule fun and lively activities; exploring a unique environment ahead brings freedom and expansion. It connects you with opportunities to mingle, and a spontaneous vibe draws a piece of surprise news and information. It opens a gateway towards a dynamic environment that offers an incredible journey.

5 Tuesday

Today emphasizes achieving stability and growing goals in your life. It brings opportunities to grow and expand your skills as you increase possibilities by being open to enriching your life. It offers new beginnings that stir creative inclinations, promoting developing innovative projects. Tapping into your ability to manifest personal goals creates rising inspiration that provides a flurry of possibility.

6 Wednesday ~ Sun conjunct Mercury 11: 08, Last Quarter Moon in Gemini 22:21

Independent thinking and innovative ideas can be attributed to the Sun, Mercury conjunct today. It opens a path that rebuilds life with a lighter hue. It sets the scene to embrace a happy-go-lucky chapter. It brings an original and creative journey that feels like the right fit for your current situation. Exploring opportunities helps you stretch past your comfort zone and grow your abilities in a new area.

7 Thursday

Things are ready to shift forward as a new opportunity crops up that lets you channel your energy productively and efficiently. You head towards growth, bringing options that are right for progression. Creativity soars under a positive influence that cultivates a unique landscape. It brings a productive and energetic time where significant change leads life forward. An influx of social opportunities enriches your life.

8 Friday ~ Sun trine Jupiter 11:12

The Sun forms a trine with Jupiter, which increases good luck and fortune in your life. A positive influence nurtures beneficial outcomes. Mapping out new options unearths a diamond ready to shine. It brings the kind of expansion and growth that cranks up potential and elevates your success rate. It sparks an evolving journey of working with your abilities and refining your skills. It opens a path that grows your world.

9 Saturday

A new priority comes into focus, which brings a refreshing aspect that connects you with your broader social environment. You strike gold and enter a winning chapter as a new companion enters your life. It brings new adventures and good fortune into your world. Sharing with friends promotes harmony and well-being. A gathering of like-minded people ahead brings lively discussions that unleash new possibilities that inspire your mind.

10 Sunday

Something flows into your life that lights up pathways of teamwork and technology. It brings collaborations and a group enterprise that gets you involved with developing your skills. You share with friends in a refreshing social aspect. It places a charming emphasis on personal growth and sharing with supportive companions. Lighter energy triggers cascading possibilities to tempt you along.

11 Monday

As you chart a course towards developing your life, you fling open the windows on a new chapter of life. An offer ahead gets the ball rolling on developing an enterprising path forward. Growth and prosperity light a shimmering way forward. Growing your talents draws dividends; it lets you blaze a trail towards advancement in your career. A new destination looms brightly overhead as life picks up speed and enters a time of rising prospects.

12 Tuesday

Manifesting happiness is on the agenda as you progress to new options that help you create magic. Exploring various avenues helps you reveal an exciting vista of pathways that grow your skills and nurture your talents. A time of discovery overhead draws options that build a path to extend your world outwardly. Your circumstances are continually evolving and changing. Moving away from areas that limit progress cracks the code to a brighter chapter in your life.

13 Wednesday

A new phase of life is coming that sees progression taking center stage in your life. It pairs you up with opportunities that head towards growth. It provides room to flex your creative muscle and dive into an expressive environment that develops unique goals. A time of learning the ropes of a new area draws expansion. It helps you break fresh ground that opens the floodgates to new possibilities. Optimism and inspiration see the potential surge in your world.

14 Thursday

Giving your goals great concentration lets you get serious about developing your life. It helps you hit the ideal alignment to grow your world. You discover a broader vantage point that offers new possibilities to grow your gifts. You certainly can create an upgrade in your life by unearthing leads and connecting with others who provide advice and support. Changes ahead nurture your talents and advance your skills.

15 Friday ~ Rosh Hashanah (begins at sunset), New Moon in Virgo 1:40, Mercury turns direct 20:20

Mercury turns direct, and this improves communication and interpersonal bonds. It offers a renewed interest in your social life that helps harmonize frazzled tensions that occurred during the retrograde phase. Sharing time with your clan offers enchantment and magic. It brings fun and excitement back into your social life.

16 Saturday ~ Sun trine Uranus 1:23

The Sun trine Uranus aspect today adds a dash of spontaneity and excitement into your life. It is a favorable aspect that brings the freedom-driven chapter to light. Focusing on your social life draws a pleasing result as you connect with kindred spirits who offer excitement and passion. It emphasizes creativity; it brings a perfect time to cook up a storm of new ideas and endeavors. Someone in your broader social circle gives you a nudge in the right direction.

17 Sunday ~ Rosh Hashanah (ends at sunset), Venus square Jupiter 6:12

The Venus square Jupiter aspect makes it the perfect day for unwinding and relaxing with your social circle. An easy-going vibe draws thoughtful conversations and entertaining ideas. It gets a chance to rejuvenate your spirit. This chapter delivers essential downtime that enables you to dip into sharing thoughts and ideas with another person who has been out of the loop lately.

18 Monday

Essential changes draw new information to light. You unearth a lead that encourages growth and progress in your life. A gateway opens that decodes the path ahead as you get a clear idea of where to develop your goals. It offers a blaze of new possibilities that help you build your vision for future growth. Streamlining the demands on your time and weeding out distractions offers rising prospects that promote tangible results.

19 Tuesday ~ Sun opposed Neptune 11:17

Your perception broadens as the Sun lights up Neptune's dreamy aspects. Engaging with creativity and imagination draws rising ideas and innovative concepts to consider. Following your dreams lets, you reach for a goal that touches your life on many levels. It brings a chance to develop your abilities and draw new possibilities to light that nurture your talents. Offering your gifts to others lets you spread your wings and grow your social circle.

20 Wednesday

It is an incredibly potent time to grow your world as you enter a cycle of increasing options. It places you in an excellent position to achieve tangible results. Setting intentions and maintaining a positive outlook paves the way forward. You take concrete action, and this proactive approach draws a pleasing effect. You soon get busy building new foundations that crack the code to a winning chapter.

21 Thursday ~ International Day of Peace, Sun trine Pluto 5:20

Being proactive enables you to create tangible progress at a good clip. Increasing opportunities offer a compelling call to action. An emphasis on improving your circumstances launches your star higher. New responsibilities offer pathways towards advancing your talents. A unique opportunity lets you strike gold by expanding your life into a new area. You turn the corner and enjoy a winning chapter of rising prospects.

22 Friday ~ Sun ingress Libra 6:46, First Quarter Moon in Sagittarius 19:32, Mercury at Greatest Elongation 17.9W

You head towards a more vibrant and active social life. A changing scene overhead leaves you feeling excited. It brings a social aspect that offers opportunities to mingle. Expanding your circle lets you embrace a more connected and supportive landscape. It leads to a busy and active time of social engagement. Life resonates as you kick off a time of lively discussions.

23 Saturday ~ Mabon/Fall Equinox 6:50

Life comes full circle; it brings new information to contemplate. It draws security into your environment, and this stability is something to be treasured. As you make strides on improving your circumstances, you tap into a busy time that opens an active social environment. It brings a networking aspect that offers new companions and friends for your social life. It paints a picture of increasing abundance, happiness, and connection.

24 Sunday ~ Yom Kippur (begins at sunset)

A refreshing social aspect ahead lets you step out in style. Networking and mingling introduce new people and experiences into your inner circle. It adds a unique flair to your social life. It gives you the freedom to be expressive and chart a course that aligns with your vision for future growth. Support and kinship bring an influence of connection into your world. Stimulating conversations draw harmony that gets a boost to your world.

25 Monday ~ Yom Kippur (ends at sunset), Mercury trine Jupiter 12:12

Today's Mercury trine Jupiter aspect brings optimism and good news. Research, learning, study, and socializing are favored. This trine is ideal for formulating new plans and engaging in future-orientated brainstorming sessions. It's also the perfect time to sort and organize; from your office, workspace, closet, or even your whole life. It brings a happy time working productively with your energy to achieve growth and prosperity.

26 Tuesday

Expansion ahead offers the chance to develop an area that captures your interest. It has you working on larger goals that progress your talents. It brings a busy time of building stable foundations and nurturing a progressive growth phase. Surprise developments ahead improve the security in your life. It lights up avenues of success and prosperity as you turn the corner and head towards lucrative options worth your time.

27 Wednesday

Change surrounds your life and orients you towards new options. Expanding options shines a light on rising prospects that bless your life. Invitations to circulate draw vibrant talks. News and information ahead light the path forward. A renewed sense of purpose drives your vision along with momentum and clarity. Building your dreams offers advancement as you extend your reach into new areas.

28 Thursday

A positive trend ahead brings a happy influence into your world. It brightens your life with a time of mingling and fun. You unpack a stellar phase of new possibilities ahead. It brings lots of opportunities to be productive and expand your life into new areas. Positive developments point you in the right direction. It gets a lucrative assignment that offers a fresh beginning. It opens the door to a new possibility that improves your world.

October

Sun	Mon	Tue	Wed	Thu	Fri	Sat
1	2	3	4	5	6	7
8	9	10	11	12	13	14
15	16	17	18	19	20	21
22	23	24	25	26	27	28
29	30	31				

NEW MOON

Hunters Moon

29 Friday ~ Sukkot (begins at sunset), Super Moon, Corn Moon,
Harvest Full Moon in Aries 9:58, Venus square Uranus 17:53

A restless vibe caused by a Venus Uranus square could undermine the security in your love life or the broader social environment if you are single. A freedom-loving vibration brings a need to be spontaneous and engage in unique adventures that change out the day-to-day routine of your life. Sharing with friends and colleagues brings lively discussions that initiate new potential.

30 Saturday ~ Mercury trine Uranus 16:56

Today's trine is perfect for using technology to keep life are supported and flowing in your social life. Communication is your passageway to a more connected social life. Being innovative and thinking outside the box connects you with diverse pathways of growth and expansion. It brings an opportunity to circulate in your wider community environment. It triggers a cascade of possibilities that see you blaze a trail towards your vision.

1 Sunday

An interested and productive mood launches a curious direction ahead. It reveals a change in your path as an ample opportunity comes to light. It draws an expressive and communitive vibe that sees you sharing time with friends. Constructive dialogues put the finishing touches on your ideas; it brings an opportunity to tweak, edit and refine plans until they take shape. It brings a green light to nurture an area of interest.

2 Monday ~ Mercury opposed Neptune 3:34

The Mercury and Neptune opposition helps you communicate your ideas and thoughts today. However, You may find work challenging as rising creativity brings a desire to daydream. You nestle into a cozy environment that offers rejuvenation and joy. It opens the doors to new dreams that connect you with others who nurture your life.

3 Tuesday ~ Mercury trine Pluto 19:20

New energy blazes through your life and lights a pathway for developing new endeavors. It brings goals that spice up your life with possibility and potential. It draws wellness and balance into your world as you capture the essence of inspiration with plans for future growth. It acts as a catalyst of change to prepare to embark on a new path forward. Thinking outside of the box sees you take a bold leap of faith into an adventurous chapter.

4 Wednesday

Life gets a shift forward that kicks off a journey of excitement. Something special makes a grand entrance into your world that brings transformation and expands your life into a new area. It lets you take a big step up to a new chapter that has you feeling enthusiastic about the prospects ahead. There is a strong emphasis on improving your world; a decision forward empowers your life as it opens the door to new possibilities. An ambitious endeavor takes shape.

5 Thursday ~ Mercury ingress Libra 12:06

Mercury can bring an indecisive vibe that causes stagnant energy. Procrastination can be an issue that delays progress in the workplace. Focusing on removing distractions and streamlining your environment can help mitigate the effect of this transit. An element of change brings restructuring that lets you sift through your options and bring goodness to the top of the pile. It provides steady progress towards developing foundations that offer security.

6 Friday ~ Sukkot (ends at sunset), Last Quarter Moon in Cancer 13:48

A lighter aspect brings change flowing into your social life. Restrictions are lifted, highlighting a way towards social engagement that rules a time of expansion and increasing harmony. You open the path towards chasing your dreams and spending time with friends and colleagues. Sharing thoughts with a valued companion is music to your soul. It draws a happy shift that enchants with possibilities.

7 Saturday ~ Draconids Meteor Shower. Oct 6 -10

Harmony comes into focus when changes emerge around your social life. It lets you move towards a journey that takes your dreams and aspirations to new heights. It nourishes your emotions and draws well-being and support into your life. Expanding your social circle draws excitement as it flings open the door to an active and vibrant chapter you can embrace.

8 Sunday

Expanding options for your social life draw light and vital energy into your world. It links you up to a chapter that beckons with excitement and enticing options. It brings a powerful time to elevate your potential and move forward, starting a new chapter. Someone reaches out to communicate. It brings information ahead becomes the currency that lets you spend big on exploring new options and making a splash on improving your life.

9 Monday ~ Thanksgiving Day (Canada), Indigenous People's Day, Columbus Day, Mars square Pluto 1:04, Venus ingress Virgo 1:06

Positive news emerges and shines a light on possible when you expand your vision. It helps build a stable foundation in your life. Having a rock-solid foundation from which to grow your world fling opens the doors to a new vista of possibility. It is fertile ground for creativity, bringing a winning chapter into view. It advances life as you remove the blocks that kept you stuck.

10 Tuesday ~ Venus opposed Saturn 6:11, Pluto turns direct 11:43

Staying open to fresh ideas brings new possibilities into your life. It kicks off sunshine and sparkle as it connects you with a social environment that is active and lively. Networking with people with similar values and ideas brings a valuable sense of support. A chapter on social engagement provides stimulating conversations that nurture creativity and inspire an influx of possibilities for future development.

11 Wednesday

You soon become busy with new assignments that provide pathways for growth and learning. A lighter flow of inspiration and energy brings a new lease on life and this bright time captures the essence of renewal. Changes ahead bring expansion to the forefront of your world. You set sail on a voyage that provides happiness and abundance. Your life moves from strength to strength as you become adept at pivoting away from negativity.

12 Thursday ~ Mars ingress Scorpio 3:59

Focusing on the building blocks of your life nurtures stable foundations. It brings a sense of peace and balance. Fostering stability in your life helps you deal with the demands of your time. It can make things more manageable by breaking them up into smaller pieces and focusing on one task at a time. You can build upon all you have accomplished and see tangible results from your hard work.

13 Friday ~ Mars trine Saturn 12:28

The Mars trine Saturn aspect today boosts your working life. It enables you to gain traction on achieving a successful result. It puts the finishing touches on your working week as you meet deadlines with ease. This robust transit gives you the strength, ambition, and perseverance to take on the most complex tasks and complete them on time. Increased productivity and efficiency get the job done. Your self-discipline keeps you focused without being distracted or discouraged.

14 Saturday ~ New Moon in Libra 17:54, Annular Solar Eclipse 17:59

A more stable landscape emerges soon. Improving your life is a big theme that sets the stage for the new potential to occur. A remarkable opportunity is ready to unfold, setting changes that offer growth and prosperity in motion. It sees you getting involved in a life-affirming endeavor that draws balance and stability to your foundations. It aligns with a breakthrough that launches a journey that creates a ripple effect of abundance.

15 Sunday

Many opportunities ahead light a path forward. It sees a time that brings emotional rewards to your personal life. It helps you ring in a successful result and achieve a happy and abundant life. A shift forward provides you with the inspiration needed to extend your reach into a new area. Growing and evolving talents reveal latent abilities. Life offers a chance to progress your skills and develop your potential to the next level.

16 Monday

A flow of inspiration arrives with a blaze of glory. It generates an exciting lead that helps you clear the decks and embrace a new chapter nurturing your dreams. Laying the groundwork creates a path that blossoms into the room to grow your world. It brings a plan into focus and sees life pick up steam. It spotlights the development of a long-held aspiration. It brings a richly creative landscape that enables you to work with your gifts.

17 Tuesday

Researching options and planning a strategy raises confidence. It helps you move forward with courage and conviction towards developing your vision for future growth. You soon get the feeling that everything is clicking into place as you reveal a unique option that feels tailor-made for your life. You trigger a journey of expanding opportunities by being flexible and open to change.

18 Wednesday

New energy flows into your world that brings rejuvenation. A blank canvas of possibilities tempts you forward. Time spent on the home front draws abundance and invites new pathways towards growth. It opens a creative aspect that grows your world by learning areas and working with your talents. You plant intentions that let you score an avenue of growth and prosperity. Effectively channeling your energy offers room to grow your skills.

19 Thursday

Something is on offer for your life soon. It brings a journey towards happiness and harmony. It lets you negotiate complexities and reach an environment that carries you forward. A transition comes calling that encourages learning a new area. It gives you a chance to develop your skills and advance your abilities. It opens to a new role that draws benefits into your career path.

20 Friday ~ Sun conjunct Mercury 5:37

In conjunction with Mercury, the Sun is a favorable aspect that attracts communication. It is the best of all elements for receiving or sending communication. Interacting with others is vital today. It stimulates your need to share ideas and engage in thoughtful discussions that nurture well-being and harmony in your life.

21 Saturday ~ Orionids Meteor Shower Oct 2ⁿᵈ – Nov 7ᵗʰ,
Mercury square Pluto 12:50, Sun square Pluto 14:09

Today's aspect causes a challenging environment as you find your judgment or authority tested. Being challenged and put to the test feels uncomfortable as you think you are making the right choices and decisions for your life. The Mercury square Pluto transit also attracts interactions with other people who feed the gossip mill and cultivate drama, leading to a toxic environment.

22 Sunday ~ First Quarter Moon in Aquarius 03:29, Venus trine Jupiter 4:32,
Mercury ingress Scorpio 6:46, Mercury trine Saturn 16:12

The Venus trine Jupiter aspect offers golden threads around your social and love life. It is one of the most anticipated transits which harmonizes interpersonal bonds and offers rising prospects of good luck to your romantic life. It is of particular interest to those seeking love or lovers wanting a deeper romantic bond.

23 Monday ~ Venus at Greatest Elongation 46.4W, Sun ingress Scorpio 16:17

Opportunities to mingle ahead encourage constructive dialogues that bring a new perspective into your life. It draws a fruitful time of positive influences that bring new options to your table. The way forward becomes bright and optimistic as you get the chance to rebrand your image in an exciting new area. It brings a mission that enables you to grow your life. It shakes up the available options and corresponds with a journey that advances your abilities.

24 Tuesday ~ Sun trine Saturn 7:13

Today's Sun, Saturn trine gives you a commanding presence in the workplace. Confidence peaks in mid-afternoon, enabling you to effectively manage the day's tasks with relative ease as your energy keeps humming along productively. You conquer the workload and achieve a robust result with your consistent and disciplined efforts, which draw a pleasing effect and the added benefits of increased job satisfaction.

25 Wednesday

Life holds glittering possibilities that encourage expansion. New options advance life towards a progressive and prosperous journey that nurtures your creative abilities. Working with your skills brings assignments that align you towards growth. A turning point offers transformation and connects you with others on a similar journey.

26 Thursday

A lovely time ahead that hits a high note in your social life. It helps you clear away limitations and expand horizons by engaging more in your community. It brings a positive outlook that ignites your imagination with fresh inspiration. It draws the correct characters into your life. It aligns you with a time of heightened activity and lively discussions. It brings sunny skies overhead as you focus on an area that holds meaning.

27 Friday

You soon transition towards a journey of great promise for your life. It does help to keep checking in with your hopes and dreams and make sure they align with the journey ahead. Making yourself a priority brings improvement into your world. Designing your life is a strong focus that draws happiness and abundance into your world. Creating grounded and secure foundations is a vital aspect of this process of reaching for your dreams.

28 Saturday ~ Mars opposed Jupiter 16: 03, Hunters Full Moon in Taurus 20:23 Partial Lunar Eclipse 20:14

You can embrace one of the luckiest opposition aspects today when Mars opposes Jupiter and draws good fortune into your life. The winds of change carry news information into your surroundings. Today's transit increases your self-confidence and ability to handle your time and energy demands. It brings a competitive edge that fuels ambitions and the desire to achieve your goals.

29 Sunday ~ Mercury opposed Jupiter 3:44, Mercury conjunct Mars 14:21

Today, Mercury is the show's star and draws a favorable aspect that nurtures good fortune in your social life. It brings a chance to share with friends and loved ones. Relaxing and unwinding enable you to restore frazzled nerves and build robust foundations. You enter a time of inspiration, manifestation, and engagement with friends. A more social aspect brings a breath of fresh air into your surroundings.

NOVEMBER

Sun	Mon	Tue	Wed	Thu	Fri	Sat
			1	2	3	4
5	6	7	8	9	10	11
12	13	14	15	16	17	18
19	20	21	22	23	24	25
26	27	28	29	30		

New Moon

BEAVER MOON

30 Monday

News arrives that lets you steam forward at a productive pace. As life becomes busier and more active, delegating brings assistance that helps you put together a strategy for success. New possibilities let you start sharing your gifts and working with your talents. It brings an opportunity to collaborate, a fruitful meeting of the minds. Sharing thoughts and ideas provide the ideal backdrop to this dynamic environment.

31 Tuesday ~ Samhain/Halloween, All Hallows Eve Venus trine Uranus 12:51

Embrace a magical and vibrant Halloween under the influence of an engaging and dynamic Venus trine Uranus aspect that adds a dash of spontaneity and fun into your life. It does let you explore possibilities as you engage with your broader community environment. It brings a productive and lively chapter that is the catalyst for growth. Sharing thoughts and ideas with kindred spirits illuminate a refreshing time of enjoying a change of pace.

1 Wednesday ~ All Saints' Day

A surge of unique options brings an optimistic vibe into your world. You strike gold as you launch forward and develop your talents. Evolving and growing on this journey helps you weather the storms and head towards sunny skies. Nurturing your dreams draws valuable results that inspire you to increase your life. New goals and an inspiring vision help you implement functional changes that offer rising prospects.

2 Thursday

A proactive approach reshuffles the deck as you head towards a landscape imbued with possibility. It brings a chance to refine and upskill your talents. Rising prospects draw advancement, encouraging you to keep evolving and growing your abilities as new horizons tempt you forward. You reawaken to the magic and possibility of working with your creativity to develop a plan for future growth.

3 Friday ~ Sun opposed Jupiter 5:02. Venus opposed Neptune 22:05

The Sun opposed Jupiter transit brings the increasing potential for wealth and good fortune. Rising prospects see things in your life fall in place as you turn a corner and head towards a lucky streak. You discover growth arrives in curious ways. It begins a quest of working with your abilities and advancing your life into new areas. Life picks up the pace, and as you gain momentum, a whirlwind of activity tempts you forward.

4 Saturday ~ Taurids Meteor Shower. Sept 7th - Dec 10th
Saturn turns direct in Pisces 7:15. Mercury opposed Uranus 16:06

The Mercury opposed Uranus transit brings a chaotic and hectic pace. The busier pace may leave you feeling tense, anxious, and scattered. Uranus adds a dash of the unexpected, leaving you scrambling to deal with surprise news. Information emerges out of the blue, leaving you wondering what will happen next. Focusing on the basics improves balance.

5 Sunday ~ Last Quarter Moon in Leo 08:37

A big reveal lets you set sail on a voyage filled with promise. Smoother sailing marks a bold new beginning in your life. It brings a time of transformation that enables you to build your world and move in alignment with the person you are becoming. It brings improvement to your personal life as you light up pathways of connection and companionship.

6 Monday ~ Venus trine Pluto 14:38

Today's Venus trine with Pluto adds intensity to your love life. This aspect turns up the heat in your personal life. Sexual attraction and passion rise as you get busy developing your personal life. Singles are likely to find new romance soon, while couples can embrace a more connected and sizzling love life. A lively and social element adds spice and excitement; a dash of adventure creates the perfect blend to grow new dreams and aspirations.

7 Tuesday ~ Mercury trine Neptune 1:36

Creativity, imagination, and innovation blaze a wildfire of inspiration as Mercury and Neptune form a trine today. Increased sensitivity to this vibrational energy attracts a boost into your world that bolsters vitality. It offers a dramatic shift that helps you quickly learn or develop a new area. Making intelligent choices leads to a breakthrough. It does encourage advancement as you head towards growth.

8 Wednesday ~ Venus ingress Libra 9:27

Exciting news ahead brings a solid focus on your social circle. It propels you towards a journey of promise and progression. Sweeping changes on the horizon bring a time of socializing that cultivates companionship. Being open to meeting new people shapes the path ahead into a journey worth growing. It places you in the proper alignment to network with friends and draws companionship into your world.

9 Thursday ~ Mercury sextile Pluto 12:16

Today, the Mercury sextile Pluto transit adds extra layers and dimensions to your creative thinking. It brings an ideal time for research, planning, and mapping out unique areas for future development. Your penetrating inquiries delve deep and help you discover any potential pitfalls and issues. Your inquiring mind places you in a solid position to grow your dreams as you do due diligence and understand all aspects around your investigations.

10 Friday ~ Veterans Day (Observed), Mercury ingress Sagittarius 6:22, Mercury square Saturn 15:07

Today's Mercury square Saturn challenges critical thinking skills and intrepid enquiring. Tensions could flare up and lead to disruptions. Miscommunication is more likely when you are not on the same page as the person you talk to about your thoughts and ideas. Focusing on open and transparent communication can help you be on the same wavelength during this challenging aspect.

11 Saturday ~ Veterans Day, Remembrance Day (Canada), Mars opposed Uranus 21:11

The Mars opposed Uranus could catch you off guard today, leading to tension in personal bonds. An unexpected tension could flare up, causing an argument or dispute with a family member or loved one. Investing in yourself spurs forward momentum that offers prosperity. Setting boundaries and removing drama kicks off a journey that draws improvement into your world.

12 Sunday

Your perseverance rewards you with new options to tempt you towards growth. Casting your net of dreams enables you to catch a bounty of potential. Lively discussions nurture your life and deepen the potential around your social goals. It brings an emphasis on building stable foundations and working effectively towards your vision for future growth. It draws a time of animated discussions that harnesses the essence of manifestation.

13 Monday ~ New Moon in Scorpio 09:27, Sun opposed Uranus 17:20

The Sun opposed Uranus transit attracts a restless vibe that gives you the green light to try something new and different. It drives a liberating chapter that offers spontaneity as you get busy expressing your unique individual melody and personality. A sense of wanderlust guides your vision as you chart a course towards exploring new leads. The way ahead is bright and optimistic as you get busy building a journey that holds significant meaning in your world.

14 Tuesday

News arrives that brings a boost. It offers a new project that places a strong focus on working with your talents. Dabbling in a creative interest helps make the most of your capabilities as your talents shine when keeping busy. It offers a purposeful and inspiring path that cultivates your skills and advances life towards greener pastures.

15 Wednesday ~ Mercury sextile Venus 12:47

A loving vibe helps you get past hump day. Today's Mercury sextile Venus adds a positive influence that harmonizes and nurtures well-being in your world. Less stress and more enjoyment grow solid foundations. Personal relationships benefit from open communication leading to fulfillment. Things change for the better and bring an optimistic vibe ahead.

16 Thursday

Staying flexible lets, you chart a pathway that takes in new prospects and information. It brings developments in areas of personal growth and expression. It brings changes that offer blessings on several levels. Stoking the fires of your inspiration widens horizons as it launches a time of blossoming creativity. It connects you to a tribe of like-minded people who support your work.

17 Friday ~ Leonids Meteor Shower November 6-30th, Mars trine Neptune 8:36, Sun trine Neptune 14:51

Under the influence of Neptune, creativity soars, epiphanies, and lightbulb moments are the order of the day. Exploring thoughts and ideas takes your creativity to impressive heights. It teams you up with a joint project that offers collaboration, networking, and communication. Weeding out the distractions lets you focus on nurturing the potential possible.

18 Saturday ~ Sun conjunct Mars 5:41

Sun conjunct Mars brings an abundance of energy and initiative, your drive to try new things increases. A desire for action can cause restlessness if not channeled and released. Let your curiosity be your guide as you expand horizons and explore new possibilities. It helps you break down the barriers that limit progress and lets your imagination loose in a freedom-loving environment.

19 Sunday

Letting your social life become a focal point draws new friendships to light. It creates a bridge towards a brighter, more connected future. It heightens potential in your social life that offers a chance for collaboration; it brings a productive time of lively discussions that support a journey of developing your world. A potent mix of manifestation, inspiration, and aspiration helps you engage with a fresh start. It establishes a grounded foundation to grow life.

20 Monday ~ First Quarter Moon in Aquarius 10:50, Sun sextile Pluto 21:26

Today's Sun sextile Pluto transit drives ambitions and sees you heading into the working week with an increased drive to succeed and conquer your goals. Feeling determined and purposeful enables you to nail your tasks quickly and finish work with energy still in the tank.

21 Tuesday

You achieve real and lasting change by focusing on growth and expansion. It's good to pull back and reclaim your energy to shore up foundations but don't forget to set off on a new adventure when the conditions are ripe for learning. Advancement is imminent, and this lets you head towards taking your skillset to a new level. It allows you to build something tangible that offers valuable rewards.

22 Wednesday ~ Mars sextile Pluto 1:17, Sun ingress Sagittarius 13:59

Today's transit increases energy in the workplace. No job is too small as you take on the lot and work towards your vision. Working effectively and efficiently towards your goals hold you in good stead. You no longer feel as though you are treading water; you begin to see the kind of progress you have been working tirelessly to achieve. It opens avenues that encourage expansion.

23 Thursday ~ Thanksgiving Day (USA), Sun square Saturn 9:46

Saturn is the ruler of honoring traditions and following rigid structures that form set boundaries. Today's square illuminates a happy time shared with loved ones, perfect with Saturn, who delights in honoring the past. It brings an enriching time for following the music. Focusing on the positive aspects ahead heightens feelings of security and well-being. It offers an abundant chapter that nurtures your spirit by drawing well-being into your surroundings.

24 Friday ~ Mars ingress Sagittarius 10:10

This transit emits a rebellious vibe that rejuvenates your energy and has you seeking expansion. It brings an empowering outlook as further opportunities arrive to tempt you along. Crafting your vision for future growth brings an environment that showcases your abilities. It releases the stumbling blocks that limit progress and eliminates doubt as you head towards life-affirming experiences.

25 Saturday ~ Mars square Saturn 16:57

Today's aspect can feel challenging as your mind is on Saturn's to-do list. You may find it difficult to relax and unwind when your thoughts turn to the irons you have burning in the fire. Adventure and excitement prominently figure as you break free of limitations and expand your life. It lets you take your situation to a new level as you reveal a journey that offers room to grow. It brings the necessary motivation to push forward towards a new area.

26 Sunday

A lovely time ahead hits a high note in your social life. It draws unique characters into your life. Sunnier skies loom overhead as you expand your life and grow your world. You soon team up with a friend who brings companionship and shares thoughtful ideas with you. Building stable foundations usher in a peaceful and tranquil environment. It underscores an atmosphere of rising potential.

27 Monday ~ Beaver Full Moon in Gemini 09:16, Mercury square Neptune 13:26

Today, the Mercury square Neptune aspect can distort or make mountains of molehills. It adds a dash of illusion into your business dealings that can have your head spinning with tall tales and trying to sort the truth from the exaggeration. This area is one of those days that tempts you to expand the barriers and think outside the box to develop workable solutions.

28 Tuesday

An emphasis on growing your world soon opens new pathways. It enables you to take on a learning course and engage in activities connected with a social environment. Creativity heightens, and it assists in taking your work to a broader audience. Contributing your talents to a group project provides the chance to share your skills with others who offer guidance and advice. Events online up beautifully to nourish your life with new possibilities.

29 Wednesday

A refreshing change of pace ahead reveals new information that offers a wide vista of possibility for your life. Being open to new options sparks inspiration. It provides functional changes that advance capabilities and promote your skills. A bustling time of crafting your vision lets you get busy with expanding life outwardly. You gain traction on developing growth. An emphasis on advancement brings a pleasing result.

30 Thursday

A positive influence ahead that helps you craft your vision for future growth and journey towards advancing life to the next level. You open a new chapter in your book of life and discover a vast landscape of possibility that is tempting you forward. Nurturing your creativity stirs up exciting options. You peel back the layers and reveal latent abilities ready for refinement as you grow and evolve.

December

Sun	Mon	Tue	Wed	Thu	Fri	Sat
					1	2
3	4	5	6	7	8	9
10	11	12	13	14	15	16
17	18	19	20	21	22	23
24	25	26	27	28	29	30
31						

New Moon

COLD MOON

DECEMBER

1 Friday ~ Mercury ingress Capricorn 14:29

A person reaches out to share news, bringing a blossoming activity. It puts new potential front and center in your social life. Laying the groundwork for stable foundations with this person encourages growth. Being open to change underscores your willingness to expand your horizons and head towards new adventures. It helps you remove blocks and open the path ahead.

2 Saturday ~ Mercury sextile Saturn 15:25

Today's Mercury sextile Saturn transit is favorable for organizing and streamlining your workload to create a stimulating and productive environment. Expressing authority and leadership skills create a purposeful and productive environment. You may want to start a vision board or a journal to help track projected outcomes. It brings the potential for professional collaborations and joint projects with others who help grow your skills.

3 Sunday ~ Venus square Pluto 13:29

Today's aspect could see a flare-up of jealousy or possessiveness. Your romantic partner may feel threatened by heightened social activities and invitations in the pre-run up to Christmas. Take time to support and boost confidence to help offset the Venus square Pluto aspect. Being aware of these fears' dynamics helps keep relationships healthy and balanced.

4 Monday ~ Mercury at Greatest Elongation 21.3 E, Venus ingress Scorpio 18:48

News arrives that invites you to an event in your broader community environment. It brings contact with people you haven't seen for a while, and this mingling and networking reconnect with what is most meaningful in your life. Thoughtful discussions nurture well-being and put a spotlight on harmony. A sense of celebration lingers long after the event as you feel lighter and more connected with expanding your life.

5 Tuesday ~ Last Quarter Moon in Virgo 05:50, Venus trine Saturn 22:51

Today's Venus trine Saturn transit is ideal for developing relationships. Self-expression, warmth, and affection flow freely under this favorable aspect. It takes you towards an active environment that improves harmony and happiness. You proceed towards a productive climate that blesses your social life with invitations to mingle. There is a surprise communication ahead that brings excitement.

6 Wednesday ~ Neptune turns direct in Pisces, 12:38

With Neptune turning direct in Pisces, an extra emotional element adds flavor to your dreams, creativity, and vision. Wistful thinking, goals, and fantasies let you move beyond the material world and escape into fanciful thoughts around future possibilities. Many raw potentials are ready to flow to connect you with kindred spirits. It helps cultivate interest in new hobbies and goals by sharing brainstorming sessions with those who support and motivate your life.

7 Thursday ~ Hanukkah (begins at sunset)

Changes overhead take you on a new adventure. It sees improvements in terms of friendship, creativity, and networking. It lets you plot a course that helps you tackle new dreams and goals. A surge of inspiration flows into your social life. It sets the stage to connect with others in your broader community. It brings a time filled with music, laughter, and vibrant conversations.

8 Friday ~ Mercury trine Jupiter 4:04

Mercury's trine Jupiter transit today ignites the possibility of heightened intuition and attracts a chance to chill with friends. You can gear up for a more supportive and connective time that enables you to network with your tribe. It brings a happy chapter that broadens the scope of potential in your world. Abundance flourishes as you nurture areas that grow your life. A social aspect ahead brings harmony and lively engagement into view.

9 Saturday

Gossip arrives that provides new information and insight into your social life. All indications are that life is about to become interesting. It does bring insight into an area that had felt troubling. An open-hearted discussion paves the way forward towards improving social bonds. It draws a sense of harmony and abundance into your world. It does bring a connected aspect that shines a light on sharing thoughts and ideas with another person.

10 Sunday ~ Venus opposed Jupiter 3:34

This astrological transit adds an indulgent vibration and has you wanting to explore hedonism, romance, and magic. The pursuit of pleasure attracts social engagement, relaxing, and unwinding with a leisurely influence restoring well-being in no time. It keeps the fires of motivation burning as you mingle with kindred spirits. It marks the start of an inspired and joyful phase. Being on the same wavelength and talking with friends hits a sweet note in your life.

11 Monday ~ Mercury sextile Venus 19:22

Communication flows freely into your social life, attracting invitations and opportunities to mingle. The Mercury sextile Venus aspect nurtures stable foundations and happiness. The tone shifts and becomes lighter; enthusiasm weaves gently through your life. It brings a playful time that lets you pursue expanding your social horizons. It does shine a light on support and conversations that create space for abundance to flow into your life.

12 Tuesday ~ New Moon in Sagittarius 23:32

There is an emphasis on improving your life that brings a transition forward. It offers options that encourage growth and delivers an enriching time that draws happiness into your world. Creativity burns brightly, bringing new ideas to explore. Life picks up the pace and becomes more active and productive. It helps you find your groove and develop a situation of interest.

13 Wednesday ~ Mercury turns Retrograde in Capricorn 7:08
Geminids Meteor Shower Dec 7-17th

Mercury turns retrograde, seeing some communication issues cropping up over the next few weeks. Plans and times quickly become mixed as messages scramble during this more chaotic planetary phase. Cutting away from problematic areas and focusing on the most meaningful path forward will draw a pleasing result that offers a brighter chapter ahead.

14 Thursday

News arrives that inspires your imagination. It helps you make efficient changes that expand your horizons. It builds social connections and draws harmony into your scene. It enables you to nurture creativity and develop friendships that grow and evolve your tribe. It brings a lighter flow and energy that supplies fresh optimism. Constructive dialogues draw creative solutions and a sense of connection.

15 Friday ~ Hanukkah (ends at sunset)

Being open to change expands the scope of what is possible in your life. It helps you discover possibilities in everyday projects, and it brings an assignment that inspires growth. Getting involved with learning and refining your abilities brings a chance to work with others who share similar gifts. It brings a triumphant time that sees your star shining brightly.

16 Saturday

You reveal information that becomes a gateway to something extraordinary in your life. Change ahead sweeps away blockages and dismantles limitations. It clears the path and creates the perfect environment to grow your world. Improving circumstances brings communication that harmonizes and rejuvenates. It draws balance and creates a grounded foundation. It opens a gateway towards a happy environment.

17 Sunday

A surprise hits the right note. It reveals itself quickly when information arrives that encourages change. It draws an enlightening perspective that gives you a fresh outlook about the path ahead. More surprises are on the horizon, bringing messages and opportunities. It marks an expressive and social chapter that puts the shine on your personal life. More security is on offer, and this brings a stable platform from which to expand your horizons.

18 Monday ~ Mercury trine Jupiter 14:33

Mercury trine Jupiter transit brings optimism, luck, and good news. Information arrives that bodes well for your social life. Indeed, it's easy to make new friends under this favorable influence that sparks social engagement and thoughtful discussions with friendly characters. It opens the gateway towards a happy environment that motivates change. It lets you progress forward at your own pace with your unique style.

19 Tuesday ~ First Quarter Moon in Pisces 18:39

News ahead cracks the code to a happier chapter. It brings a chance to reboot and rejuvenate your life. It ushers in an expressive atmosphere that offers social engagement and supportive energy. It brings positive change that improves the daily aspects of your life. It washes away outworn energy and creates space to move forward to greener pastures. It brings a time of vibrant conversations that connect the dots on a new chapter.

20 Wednesday

You open up opportunities to improve your bottom line. It lets you release outworn situations, and it brings a chance to take on a new endeavor that bodes well for your situation. It brings a chapter that has you wanting to learn, grow, and be productive. It draws an enterprising time that shines the floodlight on an area that offers room for progression. Finally, it brings news of a role that feels like a perfect fit.

21 Thursday ~ Ursids Meteor Shower Dec 17ᵗʰ – 25ᵗʰ, Venus opposed Uranus 7:04, Mercury sextile Saturn 12:35

Today's Venus opposed Uranus alignment brings growth to personal relationships. Increasing synergy and chemistry could spark a new romance or flirtation opportunity. It does let you draw abundance into your life; harmony is ready to blossom. New possibilities connect you with a blossoming path of potential.

22 Friday ~ Sun ingress Capricorn 3:24, Yule/Winter Solstice 03:28, Sun conjunct Mercury 18:53

The Sun conjunct Mercury aspect favors communication. It brings the sharing of thoughtful dialogues and entertaining discussions. It does feed your confidence; it brings a chapter that revolutionizes how you communicate and express yourself to others. You build bonds that have room to grow ever stronger. It does set the scene for more abundant energy to flow into your world.

23 Saturday ~ Mercury ingress Sagittarius 6:19

As you unfurl the coming chapter, you discover lightness and engagement with a social aspect. It brings a unique possibility to the forefront of your life. You benefit from mingling and networking with friends and companions. As foundations stabilize, you unlock the gate and head towards greener pastures. It helps you move away from storms and develop an area of interest.

24 Sunday ~ Sun sextile Saturn 17:28

Sun sextile Saturn transit lends patience to family gatherings, which can be a godsend if your family dynamics tend to be challenging. Celebrating the moment becomes a beautiful calming ritual that draws peace and abundance into your life. Continuing to improve your circumstances becomes an essential focus for you moving forward. It reintroduces you to the simplicity of happiness.

25 Monday ~ Christmas Day, Venus trine Neptune 17:15

Venus trine Neptune transit is the perfect backdrop to Christmas. It attracts creativity, well-being, and fulfillment. This transit favors singing, music, and delighting in the celebration of the day. Sharing ideas and thoughts with others marks an essential new chapter that lets you greet the future with an open spirit. It does see a theme of abundance is ready to emerge, and an enriching sense of connection lights the path forward.

26 Tuesday ~ Kwanzaa begins

Rising confidence paves the way forward to getting involved in growing your social life. Soul-stirring conversations usher in thoughtful discussions that re-energize life. You open a gateway towards a happy phase of developing your social life and connecting with others who reflect your values. Sharing thoughtful discussions fills your spirit with refreshing ideas. It brings a grounded and stable environment that leaves you feeling settled.

27 Wednesday ~ Cold Full Moon, Moon before Yule in Cancer 0:34,
Mercury square Neptune 7:36, Sun trine Jupiter 15:28

The Sun trine Jupiter aspect lights up a healing and therapeutic vibe, sending blessings into your world as it removes the heaviness. Chasing your dreams marks the beginning of a journey that enhances your circumstances on many levels. Designing your life following your core beliefs and vision for future growth becomes a strong focus. The wheels are turning, and soon you discover possibilities that promote growth and advancement.

28 Thursday ~ Mercury conjunct Mars 0:26, Mars square Neptune 22:15

The Mars square Neptune aspect brings gossip and scandal to your ears. You hear surprising news that feels disconcerting. Suppose something doesn't ring true to your ears. In that case, you should do your own investigating as this transit could draw misinformation leading to confusion. You gain a broader perception of your life. You can begin to see potential pitfalls as well as exciting possibilities.

29 Friday ~ Venus sextile Pluto 6:00, Venus ingress Sagittarius 20:21

The Venus sextile Pluto transit deepens romantic love and grows relationship potential. It brings an expressive time of nurturing a wellspring of abundance in your world. It leads to developments around your personal life. Expansion hits the ticket for an incredible journey forward. It blends creative magic with the synergy that blesses your life.

30 Saturday

Moving on to greener pastures opens your life up to unique options. Life blossoms under your attention and care as you unearth new leads to develop. Change and evolution are part of the continual cycle that deepens your talents and grows your world. Moving away from drama and areas that have become stale aligns you with a journey that ushers in new possibilities.

31 Sunday ~ New Year's Eve, Jupiter turns direct in Taurus 2:41

In a promising sign, Jupiter turns direct on New Year's Eve. It foretells bright blessings, good fortune, and opportunities on the horizon. Unlimited possibilities spark inspiration and wonder in your life. Mapping out plans helps capture the essence of manifestation to bring new prospects into your life. A new chapter of life is coming. Evaluating your options draws good fortune in the form of a new possibility. Information arrives that gives you food for thought.

Astrology & Horoscope Books.

https://mystic-cat.com/

Printed in Great Britain
by Amazon

14727716R00102